THE
ITT
WARS

Rand V. Araskog

THE

WARS

HENRY HOLT AND COMPANY | NEW YORK

Copyright © 1989 by Rand V. Araskog
All rights reserved, including the right to reproduce
this book or portions thereof in any form.
Published by Henry Holt and Company, Inc.,
115 West 18th Street, New York, New York 10011.
Published in Canada by Fitzhenry & Whiteside Limited,
195 Allstate Parkway, Markham, Ontario L3R 4T8.

Library of Congress Cataloging-in-Publication Data
Araskog, Rand V.
The ITT wars / by Rand V. Araskog.—1st ed.
p. cm.
ISBN 0-8050-0825-X
1. International Telephone and Telegraph Corporation—
Reorganization. I. Title.
HE8846.I64A7 1989
384.6′065′73—dc19   88-25109
CIP

Henry Holt books are available at special discounts
for bulk purchases for sales promotions, premiums,
fund-raising, or educational use. Special editions or
book excerpts can also be created to specification.

For details, contact:

Special Sales Director
Henry Holt and Company, Inc.
115 West 18th Street
New York, New York 10011

First Edition

Designed by Victoria Hartman
Printed in the United States of America
1 3 5 7 9 10 8 6 4 2

For Jessie

CONTENTS

ACKNOWLEDGMENTS

I thought about naming this book *Project Blue: The Defense of ITT Against the Raiders*. But Cab Woodward, ITT's chief financial officer, never liked that "color" description of our defense against corporate raiders. He was concerned that people would think we were practicing the theory that the best defense is a good offense, and that we were going after IBM, "Big Blue." Nevertheless, "Project Blue" became the code word for our defense. I found out later that the color designation came from Howard Aibel, ITT's general counsel, who so designated it as the "project to protect ITT from something coming 'out of the blue,' unknown and unanticipated," and so it was. Juan Cappello, the ITT corporate relations director, never much cared for the term—he felt it was too downbeat.

Those three—aided and abetted by the likes of Pete Thomas, Michel David-Weill, Felix Rohatyn, Jim Weinberg, Don Carter, Taylor Briggs, Sam Butler, Alan Stephenson, Walter Diehl, John Navin, the tremendous ITT Board of Directors, and my one and only Jessie Araskog—made Project Blue a winner.

They and many others played crucial roles, each doing what was required when it was required. My key staff—Kathy Condon,

Gloria Hernandez, Jim von Harz, John Chluski, Ralph Pausig, Jack Foley, Dan Weadock, Steve Csabon, Norm Prather, Charlie Hower, Norman Links, Joe Hillman, and numerous other ITT employees—made the difference when the difference was important.

My son, Bill, delivered the tough advice of a young fighter. I'll never forget his "Go get them, Dad, they don't know how to handle someone like you. They think they can buy anyone."

And my older daughter, Julie, asked, "Dad, is everything okay? Are you all right?" And from boarding school came Kathy's "Hey, Dad, read about you in *Time* magazine. All the kids are talking about it up here. You're a fighter! Are you and Mom coming to see my next soccer game?"

Make my day? You bet, they made my day!

Finally, those who helped put this book together were my very supportive agent, Michael Cohn; my editor-writer, Gerald Krefetz; and my editor-publisher, Jack Macrae of Henry Holt and Company.

All have become part of the history of Project Blue.

PREFACE

When I was seven years old, the most exciting event of my life was the day the thresher came. In early September 1939, my father had told me one evening I could get up the next morning when I heard the thresher. I could then watch it all day and have noonday dinner with the thresh crew. For the rest of the world, the invasion of Poland by the Nazis would eclipse my thresher excitement, but when I heard the thresher was coming, Poland was just a banner headline in the *Fergus Falls Journal*.

The night before—oh, it was hot—my room only had a small fan, and we had to keep the windows closed because of dust storms. The heat was almost unbearable. Nonetheless, I slept soundly, and at 5:30 in the morning I heard it! I jumped out of bed and ran to the window. The big, black tractor was coming over the hill way past Emil Olson's place—belching smoke, chugging away with the huge thresh rig rolling behind, rattling along the gravel road.

In two hours, the rig would be ready for work, run by power belts from the tractor stationed about fifteen yards from the rig. I had been warned by Dad to stay away from those moving belts— belts that could grab at your clothes and pull you in to be crushed, I was told.

By 6 A.M., Dad's neighbors began to drive their wagons, pulled by great horses, into our grain fields, where bales of grain had been piled ready for pickup. When a wagon was full, it would drop the bales next to the thresh rig and the crews would fork them into the rig for threshing. When several bales hit the thresher chopper at the same time, the tractor would groan and chug harder for a few seconds and then slow down once the bales were cleared, as if catching its breath.

At noon, I marveled at the piles of food—potatoes, meat loaf, gravy, corn, bread, pie, and coffee—the men ate. I was so proud to sit with them to eat, I didn't dare speak. They didn't say much to me. The fact is, they didn't say much to each other. They were hungry and there was still an afternoon of work to do. Most of them had milked cows and fed pigs and chickens before they came that early morning, and would have to do the same that night. It wasn't until Sunday that they would talk some, but even Sunday wasn't much of a day of rest for most of them.

The next day, the rig was gone. The great tractor had pulled it into the sunset the night before, but a huge stack of straw remained where the rig had worked. I put on my little straw hat, picked up my BB gun, and walked to the straw pile, where I sat in my coveralls, chewing on a piece of straw the way the men did, watching and listening and dreaming.

I would sit out there with my BB gun and look around, and a beautiful meadowlark would sing happily from its perch on a barbed-wire fence. I would point that BB gun at the meadowlark, sitting on that fence only forty feet or so from the straw pile. But I would not pull the trigger—I would just fake it and listen to it sing. Anyone who has not heard a meadowlark in Minnesota has missed something special. So I faked shooting the gun, and finally, after a while, a hawk would fly over, high in the sky, and I would fire away with that little gun. The BBs got nowhere near it and couldn't have brought down the hawk if they had. It was fun and it was exciting. The meadowlark was beautiful and wonderful and vulnerable. I could have hit it easily. The hawks were threatening, but I couldn't possibly hit them.

I'm thankful for the memory of those happy days and I remember how cooperation and kindness defined my young life. Not until 1983, when I was chairman of the ITT Corporation and under attack by corporate raiders, did I begin to appreciate the values learned as a member of a simple Minnesota farm family. Those values helped to see me through battles with takeover pirates and together with my West Point training taught me to prepare for war and wage it relentlessly.

In the midst of the raiders' attack on ITT, I decided to record my actions and thoughts and, later, to share the experience of an American corporation under siege, especially now when the frontal assault on mainstream businesses is one of the central facts of this decade.

The ITT Wars is the story of one company, but its implications reverberate through our whole society. It questions whether the successful restructuring of American business should be left to greedy, narrow, or occasionally corrupt financial interests. Thoughtful, prudent, long-range managers must accept both the challenge of hostile raiders and the need to develop creative solutions to current problems. If this book assists to that end, then the "ITT Wars" will indeed be won.

PART I
PROJECT BLUE

A corporation is an artificial being, invisible, intangible, and existing only in contemplation of law. Being the mere creature of law, it possesses only those properties which the charter of its creation confers upon it, either expressly or as incidental to its very existence. These are such as are supposed best calculated to effect the object for which it was created. Among the most important are immortality, and, if the expression may be allowed, individuality; properties by which a perpetual succession of many persons are considered as the same, and may act as a single individual.

—Chief Justice John Marshall

1

A New Environment

By the time Harold Geneen stepped down as chairman of the board in 1979, ITT had made more than 250 acquisitions and had 2,000 working units. Revenues had gone from $800 million to $22 billion, and earnings from $30 million to $560 million. It was the fifth largest employer in the United States, with more than 400,000 breadwinners. Geneen's methods were widely copied in other conglomerates and were taught in the nation's business schools. He was imitated, admired, and envied.

He left behind, however, a debt-laden corporation, one that was struggling to pay the bills for its many mergers and acquisitions. Worse, the company was vulnerable to corporate raiders that might come to call. And, as business conditions changed, call they did.

In the 1980s, ITT was one of the first major corporations to be targeted and subjected to a hostile bid by outside financial interests. The company was to be acquired and presumably dismembered: The sold-off units would pay for this exercise in financial manipulation—and, of course, provide the gross and unseemly profits for the raiders. When the time of troubles started, we at ITT did not realize that the company would be in the first wave of what would become a tidal assault of hostile takeovers against major American

3

corporations. The nation had long lived with peaceful mergers and acquisitions—indeed, they were responsible for creative growth and commercial development. However, the hostile takeovers and leveraged buyouts of the early eighties not only changed the complexion of the merger-and-acquisition business, but also threatened to undermine the structurally sound businesses that were the backbone· of the economy. The basic nature of the American corporation—a business entity that had served well since its inception—was becoming a plaything in the hands of conscience-less, occasionally corrupt speculators.

When the attack on ITT commenced, we had no idea of the profound changes such attacks would bring across America—job losses, empty factories, community distress, and misallocation of resources. The country is only now coming to terms with those deleterious consequences. When the attack started, ITT was in the midst of its own transformation; the raids complicated that meta-morphosis. Our energies were split, requiring us to fend off the raiders on the one hand while restructuring the company on the other. Either of these activities taken alone would have taxed our reserves; together, they created a fatiguing proposition.

In the course of this seven-year effort to save ITT in a new business environment, the company had run into most—if not all—of the problems and issues that defined corporate America in the 1980s: inflation, deflation, regulation, deregulation, an overvalued dollar, an undervalued dollar, an expanding economy, a recession, hostile takeover bids, demands for corporate liquidation, officious bureaucrats, even well-meaning but impractical do-gooders.

Furthermore, there were specific problems that seemed endemic to ITT alone: alleged security breaches, extortion plots, alleged espionage in foreign subsidiaries (especially in Chile), and subtle as well as heavy-handed political pressures from foreign governments.

The "ice age" descended on the business world in the early 1980s, as it tends to do every ten years or so. This change in climate was not ushered in by the fall of a great meteor that exploded and obscured the sun. Rather, it was a gradual shift in sentiment, a trend toward the precept that dinosaur-sized corporations would find it increasingly difficult to compete with leaner, more entrepreneurial rivals. All of the respected corporate tools—matrices, management by objectives, program evaluation and review techniques, critical path methods, theories X and Y— somehow failed to stem the erosion. There was no quick technical fix in the face of radical climatic change. Many large corporations, after years in the rust bowl, have emerged lean, mean, and aggressive. Conversely, scrutiny of the entrepreneurial world turns up a number of critical problems: shortage of ideas and commitment; too many chiefs and not enough Indians; revolving research-and-development teams; and the inability to achieve economies of scale in global markets.

Synergy—the concept that the whole was somehow more than its parts—had built ITT and the other conglomerates. In the early 1980s, reverse synergy became the fashion: The liquidation value of a huge company would prove that the parts were worth more than the whole. Thus, ran the theory, if the sum of the parts had greater value, the course of action was abundantly clear—especially to Wall Street and a new brand of financier. In the old days, when ITT was built by Harold Geneen and Felix Rohatyn of Lazard Frères, investment banking and high finance used their power, connections, and sources of funds to build, to create business and commerce. That was how bankers earned their fees and financiers enriched themselves. Starting in the 1980s—in some cases earlier, to the delight of foreign competitors—the financial world turned to disinvestment. Investment bankers found that they could make just as much money—no, even more—by tearing down and destroying what had already been built. There was no positive program, no vision of a better, more productive, or more fruitful economy. Of course, it was all done in the name of stockholder interest and progress, the restructuring of the American economy. Was it possible that corporate America was losing its way?

When I became chairman of ITT in January 1980, the trend away from bigness was just beginning to emerge. It only became apparent a few years later, when takeovers, leveraged buyouts, and hostile raids based on unique, new investment devices (one such instrument was dubbed "junk bond") became commonplace.

Initially, I was not concerned, since ITT had outstanding results in my first year. The earnings of the company had never been better. I was aware, however, that business conditions were worsening. Inflation, which had been creeping up through the seventies, reached devastating levels in the early eighties before the Federal Reserve applied the brakes and cut the money supply.

The recession of 1981–82, the most serious one in the postwar era, caused ITT earnings to fall because of lower sales, even though the company maintained market share, lower foreign earnings due to the high value of the dollar, and high interest charges. While earnings went down, costs remained relatively fixed. High interest was particularly destructive. As a consequence of the hundreds of mergers, the company had acquired a huge amount of debt, close to $5 billion. The debt was tolerable as long as interest rates remained low, but it became intolerable as the company's capitalization was highly leveraged: Nearly half of ITT's capital was debt. With interest rates and inflation cresting, with the borrowing rate at 21 percent and the consumer price index rising at 14 percent per year, the debt service was extremely onerous.

One of my first long-range business plans involved reducing that debt by selling off a number of companies. The problem remained: How could I transform ITT from what *Fortune* later would dub irreverently as "a museum of the investment and management ideas of the Sixties" into a service- and technology-oriented company of the eighties? Or, to use the apt analogy of Bob Smith, the senior vice president of corporate development and economics, "We would be trying to remove the tablecloth without wrecking all the dishes." It might have been easier if I had been a magician.

Every year from 1979 through 1983, ITT divested itself of more than $200 million in assets. Faced with the unacceptable interest charges, we accelerated divestment. By the end of 1984, the corporation had sold sixty-nine companies for close to $2 billion in proceeds. Yet still more needed to be done to reduce the interest burden. Our goal was to lower the debt to approximately 30 percent of the company's capitalization. Hindering this goal, however, was a major obstacle: ITT's tradition of increasing dividends. ITT was paying about one-third more in dividends than the ordinary industrial service company—a policy that became limiting for an expanding company with a goal of debt reduction.

Thus the need to attack the problem further. We had begun by selling the redundant, unprofitable, or just plain odd acquisitions of the earlier decades. Now we were sailing through a deceptive calm, approaching the eye of the storm. To cover the interest charges and dividends on the 150 million outstanding shares of stock, we were using the proceeds from those divestment sales. But ITT could not withstand simultaneous major downturns in several of its continuing businesses.

In the summer of 1984, ITT took sudden deep cuts in income and it became necessary to cut the dividend from $2.76 down to $1.00—a 64 percent slice. It was the most difficult management decision the Board of Directors ever had to make. The board was about to jettison years of high payouts. Dividends had steadily increased, with only one interruption, for almost fifteen years. While I thought I anticipated the devastation that would result from discontinuing such a policy, I could not accurately gauge the aftershocks. Certainly the stock could drop in value and we might lose some institutional backing and sponsorship. The market could overreact, and we might indeed become vulnerable—but just how vulnerable remained to be seen. Without dramatic action, however, the cash flow would only get worse, and I knew that could not continue. Well aware of the takeover and leveraged-buyout movement that had intensified over the previous year or two, we at first looked on in disinterested fashion. After all, who would have the temerity to launch an attack on a company consistently listed among the top twenty of the Fortune 500? We presumed that ITT was too large—who could swallow a behemoth?

The ground rules of business were also changing at an incredible rate; it was no longer enough to run a tight ship in the Peter Drucker mode. Inflation had changed all that, turning the world upside down. Instead of building capacity with new factories, which were becoming increasingly costly, it was far cheaper to buy ready-made assets or whole companies that either were reorganizing or had fallen on hard times. During the 1970s, the price of everything went up—except for common stock. In a real sense, it was inflation that started this trend toward breaking up publicly held corporations, with low market values in the early 1980s. Moreover, the public, lured by advancing interest rates, moved deposits from one account to another to obtain fractional increases in rates. Inflation caused the private citizen to be wary of tying up money for long periods of time lest it lose its purchasing power. Consequently, it was more difficult to attract funds for investment, and America's savings rate started to fall as people rushed to spend their money before it depreciated further.

At first no one had recognized the true meaning of this business trend. It was disguised under the cover of deindustrialization. Since much of American industry had bogged down due to high energy prices, an overvalued dollar, low productivity, foreign competition, and high unemployment, it was deemed necessary to break up old companies, especially ones with identifiable diversified parts. A number of economists, academics, and businessmen advocated deindustrializing before reindustrializing. They held that the United States had to be concerned with redistribution and reorganization rather than growth and expansion. In order to overcome the obstacles, it supposedly was necessary to deregulate and remove the constraints, especially in the controlled industries such as airlines, oil companies, and telecommunications. Deregulation and dismemberment of the old corporations became the order of the day when Ronald Reagan's troops took over.

Wall Street quickly turned its attention to national restructuring, whether or not it truly was needed. From there, it was a short leap to takeover mania and the shuffling of industrial assets, even the selling of America's resources.

Suddenly there was a new set of "heroes" in the world of finance—at least for a while. Prominent law firms created legal devices and court battles to overwhelm or infiltrate a corporation's defenses; clever investment bankers displayed new techniques for juggling corporate assets; unprincipled executives of some corporations overlooked their fiduciary duties to shareholders by buying them out and taking their companies private; risk-oriented arbitrageurs bid up the value of corporate shares, putting them "into play"—meaning stocks rose and dove on merger talk. Finally, the aggressive financiers who pretended interest in the restructuring of American industry for noble purposes—efficiency and productivity—had a private agenda that turned on personal aggrandizement and self-enrichment. And guess who assisted them in this process? Reputable institutions, including leading commercial banks, insurance companies, endowment funds, pension funds, and other financial intermediaries looking to squeeze a few percentage points of yield from their investments. Sprinters all, they were oblivious to the fact that their haste and shortsightedness were counterproductive. They forgot that business and industry cannot maximize profits for the long term by being concerned, primarily, with the results of the next three-month period. Whatever happened to long-term planning, development scenarios, and a vision of a future measured in years?

It was this distinguished assortment of friends, mesmerized by the flutes of the raiders, that now turned on ITT. The first week after the dividend cut we knew we were in for a serious, perhaps life-threatening fight, since the possible cast of musicians were well-practiced and stage-smart adversaries. The names are now familiar: Pickens, Icahn, Goldsmith, Boesky, Jacobs, Belzberg, Pritzker, and Lorenzo, among others.

How was it possible to start a tender offer for a company of this size, one deeply involved in secret military work for the Department of Defense, one responsible for the President's Moscow hot line, not to mention a company with highly regulated insurance, telephonic, and broadcast services under the aegis of state insurance regulations, the Federal Communications Commission, and other regulatory agencies? Was ITT really vulnerable?

The first "bid" for the company came from two of the wealthiest individuals in the nation. Both are billionaires—one from the fifty-seventh-wealthiest family in the world, the other from the eighty-second-wealthiest family, according to the business press. Clearly, they had the means. The question was, Did they have the stomach for a fight? What was bizarre was the scene of two of America's richest men trying to wrest a company from its 235,000 owners, who held anywhere from one to 3.5 million shares of ITT's 150 million shares of common stock.

After the initial "offer," the company moved to battle stations. The first offer would be followed by others. When other raiders came to call, we finessed their ploys by bluff and bravado. We were courted by major corporations and felt flattered at the attention, but we knew that their intentions were somewhat less than honorable. They, too, wanted us on the cheap. And in the fight for survival, we flirted a bit ourselves, buying that most precious of commodities, time. We could not know that inside our management we had a mole, someone who was foolishly attempting to undermine our efforts and betray us to the enemy.

2

The "Bribe"

People of the same trade seldom meet together,
even for merriment and diversion, but the
conversation ends in conspiracy against the
public, or in some contrivance to raise prices.
                                    —Adam Smith

The first intimation that we were in a new business environment occurred one afternoon in October 1983. DeRoy ("Pete") C. Thomas, then the chairman of the Hartford Fire Insurance Company, a wholly owned subsidiary of ITT, was called on by one Jerry Seslowe. Seslowe, clever and articulate, was a financier specializing in venture capital and investment banking situations. He had come as point man for two businessmen, Jay Pritzker and Philip Anschutz. Pritzker and Anschutz wanted to take ITT private.

The attempt to buy out ITT was no doubt based on some very appealing numbers. What Pritzker and Anschutz perceived in 1983 was a cash-rich, asset-rich multinational company whose market price did not reflect its true value. For all the "efficient market theory" espoused by some academic economists—the theory that the market distills all relevant information into the market price— ITT's valuation then of about $40 a share was low. Most of the time, markets show varying degrees of efficiencies. Was the stock

11

market efficient in the days before the Great Crash in October 1987, or was it more (or less) efficient a few days later? Not much had fundamentally changed, but public perceptions certainly changed— a fact that accounted for a single-day 508-point drop in the Dow Jones average. Of late, the only truths in the markets are public perceptions that known takeover candidates are more efficiently priced than other securities. But in 1983 few people thought ITT a likely candidate.

Clearly, Pritzker and Anschutz saw the apparent discrepancy and a way to profit from it. They thought they could low-ball the company with a private offer that would have given them a $20-per-share profit. To entice management to cooperate, they offered a sweetener. They were, quite simply, out to wrest the company from the shareholders, putting quite a bit of grease on the management wheels to lubricate the deal.

Pete Thomas briefed me after the visit. I was puzzled and concerned: How could anyone expect to buy out one of America's largest corporations? Who, other than another giant corporation, would have the audacity or the resources? What was the motivation of the offer—and was it genuine?

Pritzker and Anschutz had done their homework and had run the numbers. In their view, ITT was worth far more liquidated than living. The nation was about to enter a wild period of leveraged buyouts, hostile raids, takeovers, and forced mergers, and the attack on ITT would be one of the first. No company of comparable size and complexity had yet come under siege. Asset stripping was an old and dishonorable practice, but it had been practiced selectively—never on a mass scale. It had been many years since Ivar Kreuger and Samuel Insull used public holding companies to leverage their assets.

There was some rationale for Pritzker's and Anschutz's expectations, some reason to believe that they might succeed. Indeed, they probably thought they would be welcomed with open arms, since they would make the offer higher than the market price and claim to be "enhancing shareholder value." In the final analysis, they were out to enrich themselves. There was a fair amount of hypocrisy in these undertakings; nevertheless, this hypocrisy ultimately would be acceptable to some shareholders, who would make a quick buck. Even though it seemed almost inconceivable that two sharks would try to swallow a whale, that was the essence of Pete's message to me following his meeting with Jerry Seslowe.

Jay Pritzker and Phil Anschutz were unquestionably two wealthy individuals: Pritzker, the descendant of a penniless Russian immigrant, was the son of real estate developer A. A. Pritzker. The Pritzkers owned the Marmon Group (a manufacturing conglomerate) and Braniff Airlines; held a major interest in the Hyatt Hotel chain; and also had interests in casinos and chewing tobacco. With his brother Robert, the Pritzker family had an estimated fortune of $1.5 billion. Phil Anschutz inherited a large Colorado ranch where oil was discovered, and had interests in coal, uranium, real estate, and railroads. His wealth also put him in the billionaires' club.

Jerry Seslowe indicated to Pete Thomas that he and his associates had studied five companies as candidates for leveraged buyouts. They concluded that ITT was their first (and presumably most lucrative) choice. He said that his investment firm was owned by two principals, Philip F. Anschutz and Jay Pritzker, and they had discussed the possibility of taking ITT out from public ownership under the leadership of Rand Araskog and his management team. He indicated that his principals could find corporate financing, and he assured Thomas that they had additional financing available. As part of the transaction, Seslowe suggested that ITT could first acquire the Hyatt Hotel chain from Pritzker for shares in ITT, giving Pritzker a large share position in ITT before making the takeover offer. Then the offering price to shareholders for ITT stock would be about $20 per share below the breakup value estimated by Pritzker and Anschutz. The stock was trading at under $40 per share: Pritzker and Anschutz thought its true value to be much more than that. If they could entice shareholders with an offer over $40 per share, they might pocket a profit of $3 billion, conceivably much more. Finally, to make sure that the deal was sufficiently enticing, Seslowe also suggested that senior management would be allotted 10 percent of the return on the venture.

They had arrived at a profit of $20 a share, times 150 million shares: To them, ITT meant a profit of $3 billion, conceivably much more. With senior management's aid and abettance, I might liberally bestow 10 percent (or $300 million) to lubricate the transaction. My share would be $30 million—what I perceived to be a gargantuan bribe!

Pete Thomas, trained as an attorney, questioned the propriety of the deal and told Seslowe that he doubted I would be interested. He was right. After I heard Pete out, I concurred: "Pete, if the stock in this company is really worth a $20-per-share profit to the Pritzkers, then that profit really belongs to the shareholders of the corporation, not to some outside financial interests."

The approach through Pete Thomas was perhaps not accidental. Hartford Fire Insurance was one of ITT's most valuable properties. The Hartford had been persuaded to merge into ITT only after overcoming considerable obstacles thrown up by regulators, the courts, politicians, and consumer advocates in the 1960s and early 1970s. If Pete Thomas could be made to feel participatory in a major way, the Pritzker group might have had a lever to pry apart the company. But the lever was not there.

My first encounter with Jay Pritzker had taken place a year earlier, on Malcolm Forbes's yacht, the *Highlander*. Forbes had invited a large group of business executives and spouses to attend a West Point football game. Included in the group were Pritzker and his wife, Cindy, as well as my wife, Jessie, and we talked with the Pritzkers en route to West Point. I was impressed by his soft, friendly, pressing tone of voice, a little above a whisper when he chose. He watched intently as he talked to see the reaction of his words.

As was typical for those West Point trips on the *Highlander*, there were Bloody Marys in the late morning, a superb lunch, then the bus trip up to Michie Stadium. Malcolm Forbes distributed the football tickets and seated Jessie and me with the Pritzkers and himself. Throughout the game, we had opportunities to talk not just about the game but also about Chicago; about Minnesota, where Jessie and I had grown up; about ITT; and about the hotel business: the Pritzker-Hyatt chain and the ITT-Sheraton chain. The variety of topics led to a pleasant afternoon.

A year later, perhaps Pritzker assumed that I would be amenable, that our casual conversations had modestly paved the way for a mutual understanding. Whether it was based on the potential combination of the Hyatt and Sheraton chains, the need to build an even bigger business empire, or simply the lure of making a quick buck, Pritzker was interested in dismantling and liquidating a company to which I and thousands of employees had dedicated our careers. I was not about to let him and Anschutz "buy" me and our management team.

While Pete was conveying my reaction to Jerry Seslowe, I notified several of the senior outside members of ITT's Board of Directors—Dick Perkins, former chairman of the executive committee of Citicorp; Terry Sanford, president of Duke University; Tom Keesee, executive director of the Bessemer Fund; and Michel David-Weill, senior partner of Lazard Frères—of what I had done. They wholeheartedly agreed with my rejection of the offer.

Next, I brought the matter to the attention of the board's Executive Committee at its next meeting, but I also indicated that I was not sure it was over. I noted that we would have to proceed carefully, and the best way to do that was to achieve a market value for ITT shares greater than that perceived by Pritzker and Anschutz.

Making a profit on the discrepancy between true value and market price was the raiders' advantage. Their plan was relatively simple: do a leveraged buyout of the public stockholders with the blessings of management—and arrange for significant financial benefits to management as well. Offer the public shareholders more than the market price but less than a realizable value of the company after it was put on the block. How familiar that score would become, one that would be played over and over in the following years.

Seslowe's reaction to my response was one of "disappointment," but there was no indication from him then that the matter would be pursued further. I reported to our board that I had a speaking relationship with Jay Pritzker, that if he approached me, I would give him a decided negative response. But Jay Pritzker, in the next several months, did not come to me. It was only later, through other emissaries, that the depth of his and Phil Anschutz's interest in ITT became clear. They would shift from a friendly effort to get management to cooperate to a high-pressure and finally an unfriendly one.

It seemed incomprehensible that anyone would try to take on a corporation so steeped in technology, including classified military electronics, so involved in the highly regulated insurance business; one with so many assets in Europe and one with communications services under Federal Communications Commission (FCC) control in the United States. Unfortunately, Pritzker and Anschutz did not share that understanding, nor did some of those who eventually joined in their idea.

In the next few years, we came to know some of these modern-day raiders fairly well. They were from old money and new money; sometimes they acted in an outright manner, at other times they were devious; occasionally they bluffed, occasionally they backtracked. There was a single-mindedness in their pursuit of personal profit, almost a need to pile superfluous dollar on superfluous dollar. They seemed to be motivated by the idea of playing a game, and devil take the resulting damage and disruption. It has become a most dangerous game for American publicly held corporations. All too often, companies subject to a takeover are disrupted, dismembered, downsized, and hollowed out. The score is not yet in, but most takeovers seem to have a couple of strikes against them. The new combination does not noticeably raise profitability of the target company when it remains intact, and it may indeed lower it for the acquirer as the return on capital declines. In short, takeover benefits are gossamer illusions.

Interestingly enough, the raiders of the 1980s were wise enough to mask their motives with three pretended objectives: to rationalize American industry, to make it more competitive, and to enhance shareholder value. There is little evidence that the current takeover activities accomplish the first and second objectives. As for the third, except for a fillip in price at the initial buyout offering, the price of the target company's shares is as likely to go down as up.

On the current list of media-identified corporate raiders, Saul Steinberg was probably the first. But Steinberg now is more a long-term investor than the raider he was when he tackled Chemical Bank in the 1960s. When he resurfaced and went after Disney in 1984, he thought he could reorganize and rejuvenate the film and entertainment company. Since then, he has been putting money only into Drexel Burnham Lambert deals, and he does not deserve the raider label accorded by the press.

For T. Boone Pickens, perhaps the most famous of the raiders, his best days are past. At their peak, his machinations in this takeover world moved at the speed of a blind dog in a meat house. While he affected a folksy manner for the media, he was a shrewd raider, starting out as a speculator in the oil patch. From his Mesa Petroleum fortress, encircled by executive golden barbed wire, his forays on the oil companies (Gulf, Phillips, Unocal) did an incredible job of concentrating the American oil industry. While some praise him for his brilliance in knocking down the oil establishment, he has been no bargain for the economy, the oil industry, or the consumer. Ironically, Pickens grew popular running down entrenched management of publicly held corporations while flying his corporate jet in and out of his Mesa enclave.

Carl Icahn, probably the most astute of the raiders, considers carefully what he is doing and has the courage to proceed. He has also been lucky—a combination hard to beat. But Icahn has yet to prove that he knows how to run a successful company over the long haul. He seems too anxious to trade out of the likes of TWA, USX, Texaco—but what a power!

Ron Perelman, with his holding company McAndrews & Forbes, is relatively new to the takeover game. His big kill was Revlon, achieved with Drexel Burnham Lambert and a compliant outside board of directors. Then, in another move after Revlon, Gillette paid him greenmail to leave it alone, which only left that company vulnerable to further attacks.

The other raider group that ITT would get to know all too well was Irwin Jacobs and his followers. Jacobs's success stemmed largely from following other raiders: after Steinberg in Disney, after Pickens in Unocal, after Leucadia in Avco, after Perelman in Gillette. He is, in brief, a shark follower. Most of his new money came from frightened boards of directors that bought off him and the others with greenmail. Nevertheless, he could be dangerous, since he was capable of amassing formidable sums to buy up stock. He never made any of the sophisticated hypocritical noise that he was restructuring American industry, that his was *pro bono publico* work. He was out for money, pure and simple. As with other raiders, he has his own corporate vehicle for the raids, Minstar Corporation, which has not of late proved an overwhelming success for its public stockholders.

With this formidable cast of characters, why did ITT think it could win? While some targeted companies fought back, many caved in after one or two legal minuets or flew into the arms of a white knight. Some attributed ITT's determination to innocence, but we viewed it as a fiduciary obligation.

Pritzker and Anschutz as ''raiders'' were something of a puzzle. Why billionaires should bother with the takeover game boggles the mind. Clearly, they, their families, and their families' families will have more wealth than Croesus ever dreamed of if their fortunes only obey the laws of simple interest. In fact, as the war over ITT developed, Anschutz did not seem to have his heart in it.

Pritzker, however, seemed the aggressor, one whose previous business activities were less than ennobling. The *New York Times* has said that Jay Pritzker professed concern about the family's "being tagged as financial manipulators," and according to the *Wall Street Journal,* an associate once accused the Pritzker family of using "fast and loose" tactics. The Pritzkers started the Hyatt Hotel Corporation, then took it public; subsequently, the Securities and Exchange Commission (SEC) charged profiteering and conflict of interest between Hyatt and the Pritzker family. It was clear that Pritzker could be driven to pull out all the stops if the battle became fierce and if Anschutz did not restrain him.

To keep ITT on course through the battle that might come, I was to rely heavily on the top management team. The key executives included Cab Woodward, chief financial officer and executive vice president, who had previously been chairman and chief executive officer of Continental Baking Company, a major ITT subsidiary. Cab was extremely well known in the financial community and highly thought of by commercial and investment bankers.

The treasurer of the corporation, who reported to Cab, was John Pfann, a solid and loyal supporter of ITT. John was concerned about recent negative cash flow due to research-and-development expenditures, capital costs, interest payments, and a high rate of dividend payout.

Howard Aibel, general counsel of the corporation, had seen ITT through the difficult San Diego Republican convention in 1972, when some overzealous ITT employees had pledged money to underwrite the event, and through the Chile scandal of 1970, when ITT was accused of fomenting civil war. Howard, who possessed one of the most adroit and wide-ranging legal minds around, was known as "Mr. Cool."

Jack Hanway, the director of administration, managed personnel, industrial relations, security, and a wide range of other activities. Jack took an extremely hard line, but he was a loyal professional who had tremendous instinct for where the power was and what needed to be done to maintain it.

Edward ("Ned") Gerrity, senior vice president for government and public relations, was a man of many colors—a man who had outlasted deep involvement in ITT's San Diego and Chile scandals. Ned never liked to take the straightest line from one point to another; it was said that he often achieved objectives in his own circuitous way. He was, perhaps, my closest confidant, and my only social friend among the ITT management. Although he was only eight years my senior, I thought of him as I would of my father, from another generation. Ned's deputy, Juan Cappello, was a junior member of the group.

Finally, I had another powerful friend, ally, and associate in Pete Thomas, the outstanding chairman of the board of the Hartford Fire Insurance Company. Pete had sound business instincts and an uncanny ability to select superior people, and he worked well with me. In fact, I made the point on several occasions that it seemed we could almost switch jobs and things would still proceed smoothly. Pete was extremely dedicated to The Hartford, where he had spent most of his career, but most recently he was developing a much more significant association with the objectives of ITT. I relied on him to run his businesses with a fairly independent hand.

On December 23, 1983, I held a small party for these and other ITT executives on the twelfth floor of 320 Park Avenue, our headquarters in New York City. The ambience was jovial. We were closing out the year with about the same earnings as the preceding year, but with an improved debt/equity ratio, and we shared a reasonably buoyant attitude about 1984.

At that party Ned Gerrity pulled me aside and said, "Rand, on January first you will have been chairman and chief executive officer for four full years. Like the president of the United States, you are coming to the end of your first four-year term. You must evaluate it, think about it, and determine what you want your second term to be. Think about the strong points and the weak points, and what you will do to fix them. I would, certainly, want to be as much a part of making what we have done even more successful and to work with you in every way you want to strengthen this corporation.''

I was more than a little taken aback at the comparison of my tenure as CEO to a four-year term of the president of the United States. I had never thought about it that way, and I had no idea what he had in mind, but it made me uneasy. I remember telling Ned, ''That is an interesting comparison. I must say I have already been thinking carefully about next year and the years beyond, but we'll do more on that as we get into strategic plans in January and February.''

3

Storm Warnings

When Harold Geneen came on board, the old International Telephone and Telegraph Corporation was basically a collection of overseas telephone systems and production companies with a smattering of domestic firms involved in radio, television, and appliances. The original concept of the company— to be a foreign equivalent of American Telephone & Telegraph— had died with its founders, Sosthenes and Hernand Behn, in 1957. Indeed, the corporation had been floundering around in the 1950s without a clear sense of purpose. It was, in some ways, a company in search of an idea.

Geneen gave the company what it had lacked, a mission to grow rapidly and steadily through the external acquisitions of other companies. In building ITT to its present size, he used the product asset base in Europe to acquire service and product businesses in the United States. Geneen's vision and his personal energy powered the company for more than a decade of unremitting growth. The range of products was nothing less than astonishing, from Twinkies to turbines, from hydrants to hotel rooms, from radios to casualty insurance.

When Geneen retired, he left behind the greatest agglomeration of businesses ever gathered under one corporate tent. He was the conglomerateur par excellence—admired, envied, and imitated throughout American business circles—and Felix Rohatyn of Lazard Frères was the mergers-and-acquisitions man nonpareil. Geneen's greatest strength was in identifying companies, together with Rohatyn, that could be acquired without a fight. He believed that it was possible to nurture companies, supply them with the fertilizer of growth—cash and management expertise—and they would expand and mature. It was too costly and risky to start from scratch, especially if assets were available at a discount—far better to acquire a going concern, provided it matched development plans. Guided by this philosophy, most of ITT's growth until 1972 was generated through external means—the acquisition of hundreds of companies in less than twenty years.

These disparate entities had one main common element—a centralized staff management system. Geneen, along with other conglomerateurs of the 1960s and 1970s, had an overriding business philosophy that strong managers could manage anything, no matter how separate or incongruent.

Geneen's style became legendary, with staff meetings marked by critical quizzing of line managers. Perhaps it was his training as an accountant, but Geneen was certain that a candid, knowledgeable, and even a charged exchange between him and his managers would lead to the solution of difficulties that might affect the bottom line.

His program was far from simplistic synergy, as some of his critics have charged. His purpose was to build on the needs of the second half of the twentieth century, when service and a service economy, he felt, would predominate. ITT had to position itself in a way to take advantage of these business trends. Geneen liked hard goods, but he was shrewd enough to know that some of ITT's older and more traditional fields, such as defense work, appliances, and electrical connectors, were increasingly risky and competitive. In the newer service businesses, such as financial services, insurance, hotels, and broadcasting, the risks were then lower and the returns on investment higher.

It was ITT's rush to acquire these businesses that finally limited the company financially. Geneen never nickel-and-dimed over price. Some have accused him of paying too much for some companies, but his decisions were always based on a full and factual understanding of the company and its product. And he never undertook a hostile takeover. But for all of ITT's success as a conglomerate, for all the imitation and for all the seminars on Geneen's management techniques, ITT stock did not sell at a lofty premium after 1973. The price of the shares was equivalent to that of other conglomerates—at least when price-earnings ratios were compared.

ITT had expanded by an extensive use of corporate paper: It issued common stock, and convertible preferred shares as well, to the shareholders of the acquired company in return for their equity. The number of shares ITT issued under Geneen increased tenfold, to roughly 150 million shares or their equivalent.

Along with the issuing of equity came the growth of debt. By 1979, the capitalization of the company had come close to being half debt and half equity: Not only was the corporation becoming highly leveraged, it was increasingly burdened with the servicing of that debt. In 1980, the servicing charges alone were over $600 million.

To further increase cash flow problems, ITT was paying high dividends. The company had sufficient retained earnings to do so, but dividends represented another problem area.

The cost of the mergers surfaced when business turned down and expenses turned up, an unhappy combination that occurred at the end of the 1970s. Harold Geneen never wanted to sell anything, so it was hard to break the acquisition habit even after he stepped down. Under Lyman Hamilton, Geneen's first successor as CEO, the company spent more on new acquisitions than it took in from divestitures the following year. Hamilton's ambivalent attempt to trim the company was one of the factors that set the Board of Directors against him and ended with his forced resignation.

Geneen had bet on the proposition that the economy, both here and abroad, would be subject to gradual but constant inflation. Under such conditions, it made sense to be a borrower, since it would always be possible to retire debts with cheaper or deflated money. When interest rates ratcheted upward in the early 1980s, this strategy backfired, making ITT debt onerous. While a little inflation enables businesses to pass rising costs on to consumers, a lot of inflation can create major problems. Moreover, the soaring dollar in the early 1980s had an adverse effect on foreign earnings. Overseas profits were extremely important to ITT, so the result was devastating when the company brought home only minidollars.

Increasingly, the financial world was looking toward a corporation's income, its cash flow, and its return on assets. ITT was in a financial box, with a collection of disparate companies—some profitable, some not, but all expensive to maintain. Was divestiture enough? The certainty was that the future lay not in diversification, but in divestiture. It was also becoming clear that the future might not even lie with some of the businesses we might have wished to keep. Divestment was not enough. ITT needed a program to focus itself on a true course if it was to regain financial strength before growing again.

As the 1980s took shape, another philosophy began to sweep through the financial world—one that was opposite to the earlier period of conglomeration and diversification: The liquidation value of companies might be greater than the sum of their parts, or so the corporate raiders suggested. ITT would become the object of this new mathematics. Even as we tried to get the corporate course clearly defined, we had to change direction abruptly.

This new philosophy had enormous implications for ITT and the rest of corporate America. It all started quietly and slowly when Wall Street was forced to end its fixed commission rates on May 1, 1975. Brokerage commissions were deregulated and competition finally came to the home of capitalism, the stock exchanges. Faced with the prospects of competing, brokerage houses and investment banks searched for new kinds of business: Some brokers opened discount brokerage offices, some opened research boutiques, and some opened or expanded mergers-and-acquisitions departments.

With deregulation in the eighties, airlines, trucking, railroads, utilities, petroleum, and banking also were faced with new ground rules and new rivals. Only after a number of years of deregulation could the business community look back to see the value of regulation in some areas. The widespread insolvency in the savings and loan industry, the dangerous confusion and dubious practices in banking, and the cutthroat competition and near-chaos in airlines have demonstrated the need for regulation. The public has a right to orderly markets where their life savings and their safety are concerned. Some regulation helps business offer better service, with some factors then being predictable.

Wall Street was ready to tender advice to all these newly deregulated industries, suggesting ways to raise cash and spin off unwanted subsidiaries. Lowering interest rates facilitated the trend toward mergers and acquisitions, takeovers, leveraged buyouts, and hostile raids. Since it was much cheaper to buy corporate assets in the stock market or through open tender offers to private shareowners, there was little incentive to build plant and facilities from scratch.

About the only element that had remained cheap during the period of inflation from 1978 to 1982 was corporate equity, but after August 1982, even the stock market began to take off. Interest rates declined and the merger-and-acquisition race was on. Enter the years of the raider—1983 through today.

With a new emphasis on maximizing shareholder value, restructuring of public corporations became the buzzword. In 1970, fewer than 20,000 MBAs graduated. At the height of the restructuring and deconglomeration movement, in 1987, the business schools were turning out 60,000 MBAs per year, a majority headed for consulting and investment banking. Management gurus sprouted faster than mushrooms after a spring shower, and management consulting and investment banking fees levitated accordingly.

It was then a very short step to the slippery slope. Engineering and production increasingly were secondary to swelling financial careers. This was a pervasive trend throughout American industry and banking in the 1980s. There was an unhealthy emphasis on finance and accounting to produce good-looking numbers, rather than innovation and superior products. Too little attention was paid to foreign competition and long-range planning, and too much to seeking tariff relief and special investment credits. Senior management became dominated by people who had never had any line responsibility but thought they could manage anything—especially their careers. Loyalty to the company was out of fashion: The quickest route upward was by listening to the siren song of the headhunter.

Senior management paid less and less attention to what was happening on the plant floor and became increasingly concerned with so-called shareholder value. The race was on to raise share value through buyouts, restructuring, and other stratagems. In addition, the investment community was demanding continuous justification for share prices, looking constantly for special events, asset sales, or raider investments.

Foreign companies were on an export spree, as consumers expressed their preference for imported goods. Moreover, foreign suppliers targeted some American industries to increase market share. American industry was finding it increasingly difficult to compete. Our foreign trade balances deteriorated seriously as the dollar climbed disproportionately to other currencies. When the dollar fell in the mid-eighties, the trade deficit was slow to come down.

In the eighties, the devitalization of industry, plus massive federal debts and foreign trade deficits, was accompanied by increases in corporate debt and reduction in corporate equity. The move to deregulate and to remove any competitive constraint—spurred on by the supply-side economists—compounded the violent speed of restructuring. The Reagan administration aimed at rejuvenating the economy by removing bureaucratic bottlenecks, and it partially succeeded, but it also unleashed a formidable material appetite in the raiders and their support services in the financial and legal worlds. We citizens would soon find out just how far afield our nation would go in the name of rationalizing business and deregulating industry. The catalysts of deregulation would leave skeletons behind, and we were determined they would not be ours.

It was this radically new business environment that ITT had to face in the 1980s, and, like most every major American corporation, the firm was initially ill prepared to cope with it.

Fortunately, we had started to unburden ITT of money-losing subsidiaries in 1979, when Rayonier took a major write-off, a loss of more than $300 million on its Quebec pulp mill. The mill had never been profitable, and it had always been costly to operate. With a glut of pulp throughout the world, its prospects were grim. The Rayonier Port Cartier mill was the first major holding to be spun off, reversing the trend of two decades of business acquisitions. It was a necessary start if ITT was to control its cash flow. Within a year, the remainder of Rayonier Canada properties were sold, but the U.S. properties were retained. Nevertheless, ITT was still paying out more than $1 billion in interest and dividends. Clearly, more would have to be done to reduce that burden. Our plan to reduce the debt to 30 percent of the company's capitalization would go a long way toward restoring financial health.

Reducing our carrying charges was necessary, but equally so was a strategy to focus our businesses to meet the challenges of the remaining years of the twentieth century. Geneen's original view that ITT should be a product- and service-oriented company was to be proved correct. After all, that was Sosthenes Behn's original impetus with the acquisition of AT&T's telephone-operating service companies and associated telecommunications product companies. The mix had changed when foreign governments nationalized the operating service companies, leaving ITT with many manufacturing firms. Geneen had to get ITT back to its service roots on one hand, while fashioning a game plan to exploit the considerable technological resources on the other.

In my time, it was important to maintain ITT's international character, since that represented a major source of income as well as goodwill and power, but it was equally important to reduce some of our foreign exposure and prune some dubious overseas holdings. We did so, selling more than $1 billion worth of companies in Europe between 1980 and 1983.

ITT's sales and earnings had crested in 1980 and then slowly began to fall for the next few years. What did not go down in a comparable way were the expenses. We were harvesting the reverse side of all those acquisitions, that aspect of the conglomerate business that made ITT the company it now was, servicing debt.

In the fall of 1983, our plate was still full, but we were better focused. ITT had promising yet costly opportunities. Earnings for the year were lower than in 1980, a record year, and the much-publicized and very promising System 12 digital telecommunications switching system was at its most expensive and critical stage of development. Having been successful in Europe, its American introduction was running into towering development costs and strong competition. The Hartford and the ITT Financial Corporation were both meeting their budgets, however, and becoming the strongest income performers for the company. This was important in order to balance the telecommunications expenditures and the debt and dividend payments.

There were storm warnings, but at the company we felt we had a good chance to avoid the most dangerous elements of that storm.

4

The Wars of Succession

Four years earlier, when I had succeeded Harold Geneen as chairman in January 1980, there had been a deceptive serenity in the company. The sense of well-being was to last for another three years before we entered rough economic weather. Back then, the peace was most welcome, a respite from the anxieties of a period of interregnum—the wars of succession had racked the company. The Board of Directors had been edgy and unhappy with the direction of the corporation, and with Geneen's delaying tactics in searching for a successor. They had insisted on his retirement at sixty-five in 1975, but he outmaneuvered them. He had groomed no successor acceptable to them. The jockeying for power intensified. Indeed, Geneen was not above adding to the intrigue, with a sparkling twinkle in his eyes.

In that bygone period there was little fear of outsiders capturing the throne. Corporations were rarely threatened from unfriendly financial interests, and golden parachutes were still an idea of the future. Leadership transitions were largely internal matters. Geneen had set up the Office of the President in 1968 to see how a select number of heirs apparent acted and interacted. It clearly centered all power on Geneen; the other members of the Office of

30

the President were more staff than line executives. It was a dilatory step on Geneen's part—he had no wish to hasten his own departure.

I was promoted to the Office of the President in June 1976, along with Lyman Hamilton, then the corporation's treasurer and chief financial officer. The corporation had a number of power centers represented by large operating divisions and subsidiaries, and there was understandable but considerable friction between line executives and staff executives. Geneen's operating style encouraged participatory and confrontational management with open discussions by a hundred managers at mass seminars. However, the execution of policy was somewhat erratic, since lines of authority were often confused when the policy was not being implemented personally by Geneen. He had retained the title of chairman, in addition to being chief executive officer.

My appointment put me into the race to replace Geneen, but at least a lap behind the other new member, Hamilton. The president's office already had two executive vice presidents and a president representing different aspects of ITT. The president, appointed in 1972, was Francis Dunleavy, a shrewd politician and at one time the successful head of the company's European operations. As one observer noted, "Dunleavy was the perfect successor—for a man who had no intention of leaving."

The two executive vice presidents were Richard Bennett, an engineer with a strong background in sales, and James Lester, who had dealt with the Hartford Fire Insurance Company and overseas management activities. While all had come from different companies within ITT, they had been working under Geneen for a number of years. Though they were younger than he, they were identified as adherents to his style. When Hamilton and I were added to the Office of the President, it was widely presumed in the company that the race for Geneen's mantle was strictly between Lyman, the darling of the financial community, and me. Lyman was the odds-on choice.

Geneen did not encourage an entrepreneurial bent among his top executives. He inspired it in the field, but it was his own province at headquarters. Whatever leadership capabilities and vision the three long-termers possessed, they had been eroded by years of subsidiary roles. As a company historian has written, they "had become accustomed to . . . taking orders from a strong, demanding and often harsh leader." There was much to learn at "Geneen University" if you were a field line executive, as I had been, but independence of thought and action were not high on the curriculum at the "university's" headquarters.

Nevertheless, in the late 1960s it was assumed that Dunleavy, Bennett, or Lester would ascend to the chairmanship to ensure continuity and stability. The Board of Directors wanted continuity and retention of the Geneen management principles, but it also wanted change. This seeming contradiction arose from the simple fact that ITT had been extraordinarily successful through 1971 under its renowned leader.

Even though ITT was part of the conglomerate movement that developed in the 1960s, it was always sui generis, with an international character that obliged it to be positioned with foreign manufacturing facilities and service bureaus. At first Geneen was not interested in acquiring other companies. When he took command in 1959, his managerial instincts concentrated on efficiency, productivity, economy, and financial performance. For the first few years of his leadership, ITT was on a shakedown cruise—an attempt to remove all the disjointed pieces and redundancies that had accumulated like barnacles over the years, while at the same time to streamline and restructure procedures within the component companies.

ITT had passed $1 billion in revenues the previous year, and Geneen's new management techniques had brought accolades from the media. He was beginning to look for new worlds to conquer. In fact, he established a task force to pinpoint acquisitions in 1963 and before long was on a shopping binge.

Geneen, encouraged by André Meyer and Felix Rohatyn of Lazard Frères, had concluded that it might be faster and easier to achieve size by external acquisition rather than through internal development, and ITT started its growth through these acquisitions. In this stage of his stewardship, no one built better or had a more adroit sense of fit and value. Once he got going, Geneen started to acquire companies rapidly—about one a month. Along with a number of small companies were a host of significant ones— Cannon in electrical connectors, Gilfillan in airport surveillance, General Controls in automatic devices, Bell & Gossett in industrial pumps, Nesbitt in ventilation, a number of companies in consumer finance and insurance, Avis in car leasing, Howard W. Sams in publishing (Bobbs-Merrill), Pennsylvania Glass Sand in raw materials for glass and filters, Levitt in housing, Continental Baking in foodstuffs. Geneen also made a serious attempt to acquire the American Broadcasting Company. Some companies were to be a nucleus of a new division, while others complemented businesses already in hand. Geneen had little trouble wooing companies—he could charm most everyone, and he promised them a heaven-on-earth in the arms of ITT. Later they were to realize that heaven was accessible only through hard work.

The board's desire for change came before Geneen passed the age of sixty-five. ITT suffered a couple of devastating black eyes in the early 1970s—not so much for what it did as for what it was perceived publicly to have done. In 1971, shortly after ITT's annual meeting in San Diego, overzealous company executives in the public relations department promised a substantial contribution to the City of San Diego on behalf of the Sheraton Hotel Corporation for assistance with the Republican convention there. Although this was unconnected to the settlement of an antitrust matter against the corporation for its acquisition of Hartford Fire Insurance Company, the timing of the contribution and the settlement looked highly suspicious. While there was no linkage, ITT's irrepressible and outspoken Dita Beard, a member of the Washington public relations staff, allegedly wrote a memo that made it look like there was tit for tat. The memo reached the press and there were questions in Congress, but in the final analysis there was no payoff, no trade-off.

The corporation had received a great deal of unfavorable publicity, and ITT was indicted in the press, which in turn tarnished the image of the company in the public's eye. Geneen might have been a master conglomerateur, but he also began to look like a master manipulator.

It was not hard for the company to lose its standing as a dynamic, aggressive force as the decade of the seventies moved to its central years. In the popular mind, business and businessmen had gotten out of control, had usurped an unfair share of political power, and were providing selfish and mindless leadership. The Vietnam War, though not initially blamed on commercial interests, eventually was viewed as benefiting only defense contractors, chemical manufacturers, and armament makers.

As the reputation of businessmen fell, youth in the country became increasingly disenchanted. One gauge of that resentment was the dramatic decline in student enrollment in business courses and business schools. It is hard to imagine now—a period in which perhaps the most popular courses and degrees are in business—but the creative energies of the young were certainly not focused on business careers in the 1960s and early 1970s. Business, simply, was out.

There was also a strong feeling that business had become too big. The issue of bigness was not new to America: Throughout our history, populist sentiment has periodically called for regulation of size, market penetration, and types of combinations. The iron and steel empire of Andrew Carnegie, the railroad cartels of Cornelius Vanderbilt and J. P. Morgan, the oil monopoly of John D. Rockefeller sparked legislation to regulate their enterprises and reduce their overreaching power. In the conglomerate era of the 1960s, a similar response was heard as bigness was denounced.

Even during the Nixon administration, the outcry against bigness was so intense that Richard McLaren, appointed to head the anti-trust division of the Justice Department, became an activist and filed suits against ITT's acquisitions of Grinnell Corporation, Canteen Corporation, and Hartford Fire Insurance Company. The Hartford was the nation's sixth largest property, casualty, and fire insurance company. It had $2 billion of assets, premium income of $1 billion, and surplus capital of $400 million. Clearly, The Hartford was a highly desirable acquisition for ITT.

Just as clearly, the Nixon administration had grave reservations about conglomerate activity, since conglomerates were making friendly acquisitions of old, established businesses. However, there was great ambivalence in the Justice Department about the proper course of action. Conglomerates were feared in the business community, but so too was reckless antitrust litigation. The antitrust action against ITT was conditioned by all these forces—fear of bigness, suspicion of conglomerates, and the hostility of established managements of traditional companies.

The antitrust impasse was resolved in 1971 by a consent decree that allowed for the acquisition of The Hartford, but it prohibited, without specific Department of Justice approval, any further domestic acquisition for ten years if the acquired company had assets in excess of $100 million. Furthermore, ITT was ordered to sell Avis Rent-a-Car, Canteen Corporation, and the Levitt home-building companies.

There was to be a limitation on bigness for the time being, but the issue was far from settled. It would arise less than a decade later, at the end of the 1970s, when American business was faced with foreign multinational corporations with immense financial resources, often backed by sovereign governments.

But in the earlier period, "Small is beautiful" was the popular cry: Even a Republican administration had to acknowledge the public pressures against unlimited size. Although ITT was the first to be affected by this renewed interest in circumscribing corporate expansion, the Justice Department had developed an antitrust case against IBM, which was subsequently dropped, and one against AT&T, which was concluded with another, most significant consent decree. In that instance, "Ma Bell" was broken up to form seven regional "Baby Bells," in addition to the original, but much reduced, parent company. Whether deregulating and downsizing the telephone system has improved service and provided economic growth remains an open question.

Other conglomerates were not so fortunate. In fact, many of them were jerry-built, pastiches of disparate parts without any rhyme or reason. For every Textron and Litton, conglomerates that were built well, there were companies such as Gulf + Western, LTV, Kidde, Avco, and U.S. Industries, which were little more than a collection of unrelated "profit centers"—in the argot of those days. And, as might be expected, the various Potemkin villages fell apart as the conglomerate movement matured. There was no guaranteed profit from being a conglomerate.

Initially, the movement did mark an essential sea change in the nature of the American corporation. Indeed, it is plausible to suggest that some of our present troubles in the mid- and late 1980s— the reckless restructuring of corporate affairs, the crazed takeover game, the flowering of greed, the weakening of competitive enterprises, the rise of foreign, state-sponsored multinationals—all had their roots in the earlier conglomerate movement. Conglomerates refocused the energies of corporate America, and not always for the better. Industrial companies into the early 1960s were, by and large, dedicated to singular pursuits, however broad those fronts might be for major corporations. In the generation just after World War II, car makers were not interested in acquiring electronic firms, and oil companies saw no virtue, or profit, in running retail catalog stores.

But the new conglomerate formations were alluring for a number of reasons: Other diversified companies might counter the adverse business cycles of one's own industry; provide an outlet for excess cash; embellish an old, staid company by adding a glitzy new technological firm; command better terms due to economies of scale when dealing with suppliers; and, not least, thanks to the magic of language, transform a mundane household appliance manufacturer into a producer of "life support systems," and a diaper service into a division called the "juvenile pollution control center."

Finally, there was the financial incentive. Shares of the new conglomerate often sold at proportionately higher prices than those of the plain industrial corporations. Overpriced shares could be used to acquire still more companies. A conglomerate was a cornucopia of endless delights—a kind of perpetual-motion machine.

ITT was one of the most successful conglomerates of the period, but even it was to run into trouble. The trend in conglomerates waxed in the 1960s, but waned in the 1970s. When the lure of the conglomerates faded, it was partly due to the overreaching of some financiers who bought companies totally indiscriminately. At one point, Charles Bluhdorn of G+W, one of the first conglomerates, was operating zinc mines, manufacturing auto parts, producing motion pictures, and rolling cigars. A washing machine company had acquired a chicken-brooder maker, an aircraft company bought a coffin and casket maker, and a chemical manufacturer bought a company that produced synthetic sausage skins. The lack of focus did not inspire confidence, since many of the conglomerateurs were shrewd buyers but inept managers—like the corporate raiders of today.

The diversification did not increase stability, enhance or multiply earnings—the raison d'être for their creation. The much-touted synergy, the bon mot of the conglomerate era, by which $2 + 2 = 5$, was a provocative idea, but too often it equaled 3. As many lost their credibility, the more narrowly focused companies came back into favor, companies whose earnings were somewhat more predictable. They stuck to one line, and they were easier to understand. Furthermore, the new entrepreneurial firms in computers, automation, robotics, genetics, communications, and defense were far better at selling an image of the future, since they often were on the cutting edge of high technology.

Some poorly managed and ill-conceived conglomerates faded

from the scene, while others continued to pursue their activities abroad to become exemplars of transnational companies. ITT had long been abroad and was generally accepted, but many of the newer multinationals presented an American challenge to local corporations and cultures. The fear of American domination in electronics, chemicals, petroleum, and other areas as a result of the formation of the Common Market led to resentment, restrictions, and a counterattack in the late 1970s from European and Japanese multinationals. Americans would not be the only ones to invest heavily in foreign countries and receive in return a flow of royalties, profits, and dividends. The present-day buying up of America is a problem whose origins go back a decade or more. None of us knew at the time that the new, amorphous business form would cast a large shadow in the restructuring of the modern corporation.

The second major public relations disaster for ITT was Geneen's involvement in the Chilean imbroglio. ITT had obtained control of the Chile Telephone Company in 1927, so the company's interest in Chile was longstanding. By 1970, CTC's interests were valued at $153 million, ITT's largest telephone property in South America. Indeed, it was now the last property; all the others had been nationalized. Geneen viewed the potential election in 1970 of socialists, communists, and splinter left-wing groups as a threat—first in Latin America, then in lending legitimacy to communism-by-election throughout the world.

Geneen voiced his reservations to ITT director John McCone, a former CIA head, who in turn contacted Richard Helms, then the director of the agency. Geneen was informed that the United States was not backing any candidate in the Chilean election. However, a private meeting was set up between Geneen and the head of the CIA's clandestine services in the Western Hemisphere—for the purposes of exchanging information. Unhappily, the official reported to his chief that Geneen offered a "substantial fund" to the CIA. He was turned down, the official noted, and Geneen testified he had no recollection of the alleged offer, but it was later to haunt both Geneen and ITT.

The U.S. Government at this point began to formulate a plan against Salvador Allende, but Geneen did not back it. It was a case of too little too late—Allende won in October 1970, and less than a year later, he took control of Chile Telephone without formally expropriating it. His informal action was presumably intended to prevent ITT from filing a claim for the value of its investment with the newly created Overseas Private Investment Corporation (OPIC), a U.S. government vehicle that insured ITT's investment against expropriation. Significantly, ITT's other interests in Chile, which included a telecommunications factory and two Sheraton hotels, were left untouched.

After the takeover of Chile Telephone, internal ITT memos, largely written in 1970, were leaked to the press. The memos suggested a variety of contingency plans to forestall Allende's inauguration. Although ITT's activities and plans seemed confused and contradictory in these memos, much was made of them. There was clearly a difference between "staff thinking" and "policy determination," as noted later on by McCone. That is what staffs are for, he said—"to think up alternatives, and then that is why you have bosses to make the decision."

It is an interesting footnote to history that Allende, whose life ended with the September 1973 coup of General Augusto Pinochet, was hardly the saint subsequently pictured by the media, but a crafty and cunning politician surrounded by a group that included several clever radicals. ITT's negotiations with Allende for compensation for the telephone company takeover had been frustrating. Allende offered to pay slightly more than $12 million for the property, far from the $153 million the company was worth. Allende was no doubt scheming to let the U.S. Treasury pick up the tab through OPIC. Later, a panel of U.S. arbitrators ruled that OPIC was liable under its insurance policy. With OPIC's help, ITT settled the nationalization matter for $125 million.

Indeed, ITT's image had suffered greatly from the San Diego and Chilean fiascoes. It was alternatively viewed as either a Machiavellian force, capable of global manipulation, or a stumbling giant incapable of getting out of its own way. The back-to-back San Diego and Chile incidents took a heavy toll on company morale.

Harold Geneen was moving into the second of his three phases as captain of the company. After the first brilliant fourteen years from 1959 to 1973, the next stage revealed an embattled commander surrounded by brushfire wars. There was no question of his competency, but he now had to deal with some self-inflicted wounds. The intensity of the battle was beginning to show both on Geneen and on the management of ITT.

The CIA connection pursued ITT for many years. Even though I knew nothing of Geneen's alleged involvement in the Chilean affair, I did know something of the CIA, since I had previously worked for the National Security Agency in Washington. In subsequent years, the CIA on three separate occasions did attempt to recruit ITT for some of its operations. And on three occasions they were turned down. The country has a right to protect its national interests, but in a democracy those activities (except in extreme, extraordinary circumstances) should be public. Every time the CIA "unofficially" came calling, I could only think of Mark Twain's cat, which sat down once on a hot stove, but never again sat down on a hot one, or, for that matter, a cold one either. We were not about to be burned again.

The CIA does no service to itself or to the business community by attempting to recruit companies to do their bidding. Public corporations should not be involved in covert activity. Invariably, the companies are left twisting in the wind when it becomes known they were involved in extralegal affairs. They are, of course, disingenuously disowned by the powers that be, and few people believe the firm's protestations of innocence, simply because someone is always willing to overreach his charge.

ITT has always had exceptional information-gathering capabilities since it operated in more than eighty countries. While the corporation increasingly functions in a fishbowl, as much as possible, information is shared on a need-to-know basis only. Inevitably, government agencies want everything—whatever is "nice-to-know," rumors, and gossip. Public corporations have no place in passing on innuendo, inferences, and hearsay, at home or abroad. Perhaps if we had paid more attention to our primary interests, we might have avoided stepping on our own toes.

ITT was at one of its critical high-image crossroads: From a company that seemingly could do no wrong in the 1960s, it was now shuttling from one exposé to another. San Diego and Chile were the most prominent faux pas, but there were a host of lesser events that undermined the public's confidence: the antitrust challenges and consent decree; the IRS's announcement of its reconsideration of the 1969 tax-free merger ruling in The Hartford acquisition and its subsequent revocation in 1974; the government's refusal to pay the OPIC insurance claim over the loss of the Chile Telephone Company; and naturally a slew of derivative stockholder suits against management for alleged wrongs. All took their toll. In 1973, the price of ITT common stock hit a record high of 67⅜. As the problems multiplied and confidence ebbed, the price slid dramatically with a general fall in the market—to $12 at the end of 1974. Geneen's magic was not working well; the string of fifty-eight consecutive quarters of 10 percent profit gains ended. However, he received a new two-year employment contract, which would take him just beyond the normal retirement age of sixty-five. The fortunes of the company were fading and there was no new certain leadership in sight.

The Board of Directors was looking for a change, but it wanted to retain the ITT management system. This paradox kept the board from moving forcefully until action was mandated by malaise, low morale, the decline of technological innovation, and a weakened leader distracted by hostile political fire from Washington. But that action would still not occur for another year or so. Only in June 1976, when Geneen was in the final caretaker phase of his career, did the board become impatient and force him to bring in two new contenders. The directors told Geneen that they would decide which one of the two would succeed him.

Unfortunately for me, and unknown to me, the outside directors had given themselves only six months to decide between Lyman Hamilton and me. Lyman had been on the Board of Directors for several years, and even in June of 1976, I was not appointed to the board. It was clear that a herculean effort lay ahead if I was to have any chance.

5

The Company at War

The Vietnam War changed the way ITT and other American firms subsequently did business. The demands of a foreign engagement—coupled with its needs for supplies, communications, and controls—brought a great many companies into the export arena. Vietnam and surrounding countries needed earth-moving equipment and telephone systems, small-caliber ammunition and floating dry docks. American military forces required virtually everything from razor blades and jungle boots to flak jackets and fire-fighting equipment. Southeast Asia was deluged with exporters, salesmen, agents, middlemen, and a panoply of support personnel. Napoleon's army might have marched on its stomach, but today's modern army requires light beer and transistor batteries.

The rapid deployment in Asia created unrivaled opportunities—opportunities that some companies exploited without regard to commercial decency or national honor. As an international corporation, ITT had long been aware of the temptations of operating in other jurisdictions, and the company had taken steps, not always successfully, to lay down guidelines and operating procedures for its overseas business. Other companies, newer to the export business, were often misguided and believed that when in Rome do what is feasible, if not outrightly criminal. The Vietnam era unleashed a wave of overseas corruption and suborning that reached from the customs clerks to the highest levels of government, such as Prime Minister Tanaka in Japan and Prince Bernhard in the Netherlands. The effect was devastating, both for what corruption did to the offending company and for the overseas perception of American business techniques. When Congress passed the Foreign Corrupt Practices Act somewhat later, it ended the dual standard and leveled the playing field for domestic corporations. In the decade since its passage, it has not placed American companies at a disadvantage—contrary to complaints of some earlier critics.

I became directly aware of the foreign pressures while spending time visiting overseas installations and foreign subsidiaries. After working my way up through ITT's defense communications division, at thirty-nine years of age I became corporate vice president of ITT in charge of one of its major groups of companies, the Defense Space Group—a job that was one of the most interesting in ITT. It extended from maintenance of the Ballistic Missile Early Warning System (BMEWS) across the northern Arctic to management of some of the most important avionics and electronic-warfare programs of the Defense Department, particularly Air Force electronic countermeasures for the B-52 and Gilfillan SPS 48 radar for navy ships. Ten companies reported to me: our defense space activities, ITT Cannon (a well-known connector company in Santa Ana, California), and the Cable Hydrospace Division in San Diego.

Early in 1972, Joe Abbott, our division public relations director, and I toured the Distant Early Warning (DEW) Line, a companion system for aircraft to BMEWS, in the Arctic north, flying from blizzard to blizzard and camp to camp with no sunlight over a period of seven days. We finally arrived at Point Barrow, a depressing outpost. What the United States Government had done to the Eskimos there was unforgivable.

Gone were the dogsleds and the beautiful huskies, except for show purposes. In their place were snowmobiles and alcohol in abundance, thanks to our glorious welfare program. Many of the Eskimos we met seemed to be intoxicated, barreling along in their vehicles. When I visited with the young, progressive, University of Chicago–educated American mayor of Point Barrow, I wondered aloud how much more damage we could do to a once-happy way of life. He could only glare at me.

Still, it was interesting to see the performance of ITT personnel under such extremely adverse conditions. Only a rare type of person would be willing to be imprisoned in a sunless environment for several months throughout the winter inside the Arctic Circle. Their only companions were records and tapes. Movies occasionally were flown in, and recreational activity almost always occurred indoors because of the constant threat of bad weather. It was necessary to follow ropes from building to building when the wind was sweeping the swirling snow, obscuring lights in buildings only a few feet away. We were impressed by the stamina and courage of our men who endured such a bleak environment and still performed so well. Ned Gerrity, always on the prowl for promotable stories, reported our trip, in glowing terms, to Harold Geneen.

A month or so later, Joe Abbott and I made another important visit—this time to Vietnam, at the beginning of the height of the war. ITT's Federal Electric Corporation (FEC), one of the ten companies for which I was responsible, had about 1,500 employees in South Vietnam, maintaining electronic communications being used by U.S. forces there. I went to Vietnam as a confirmed "hawk," believing that the United States had some rather special national interest to protect in Southeast Asia. Moreover, I believed that we should support democratic governments wherever they flourished.

Only afterward did I realize that for all our overwhelming strength, the United States could not be the world's policeman. There had to be limits to our commitments. Furthermore, the Vietnam situation was a civil war. It was almost inevitable that we would be detested by both sides.

What I saw in Vietnam was difficult to take, especially for a West Point graduate: officers' clubs for generals; officers' clubs for colonels; officers' clubs for majors and clubs for noncommissioned officers; generals keeping their wives in Thailand and commuting from the war on weekends. There was even an officers' club at the Saigon military airport with a whorehouse. Just go through the purple door, they said. I tried to, just to see it, of course, but Joe Abbott yanked me back.

Rats crawled through the best hotels and around the best restaurants in Saigon. It was hard to enter a hotel elevator without spotting a beautiful prostitute who had flown in from some part of the world to make quick money. The place was sick! Army trucks barreled down the road, driven by civilians who had stolen them within the previous few days. The only encouraging aspect of Vietnam was its children—the schoolchildren running in the streets to go to school, holding hands, laughing, wearing spotless white or blue clothing. They were the happy future of Vietnam, if only it could become free—which, of course, it did not.

In order to inspect our facilities on a mountaintop at Vung Tau, we took a helicopter flown by pilots who acted as if they were under the influence of drugs. They almost killed us, clipping treetops with their propeller blades on takeoff and landing. Heavily armed, with machine guns pointing out of both sides, the helicopter flew at high and low altitudes, depending on the nature of the terrain and the locations of the enemy. But the biggest threat to our safety seemed to be right there in the cockpit.

We spent a week in Vietnam, meeting with several general officers and expressing dissatisfaction with the evacuation plans for the FEC employees there. We received assurances that those plans would be upgraded and that they would be implemented properly in the event that the expected Tet Offensive was successful.

I left Vietnam as a confirmed "dove." Not only were we not

winning the war, but the conflict and conditions were doing irrep-
arable damage to the morale of our armed forces. Armies sent to
fight should be given a clear mandate, they should fight to win,
and they should fight with the wholehearted support of the public.
Anything less breeds contempt, ensures defeat, and makes sorry
and unforgivable use of America's youth.

Unknown to me at the time, Ned Gerrity played up my Vietnam
visit in a most constructive way: Information on trips to the field,
and the way personnel in the field reacted to me, went directly to
Harold Geneen. When I sponsored a special kind of quality sem-
inar, which received some newspaper attention in New Jersey, Ned
Gerrity made sure that all of the favorable reviews reached Harold
Geneen's desk. He made sure I was invited to all of the annual
meetings from 1972 on, so I could become known to the ITT
directors. I attended every one. He made sure he kept me in Mr.
Geneen's view as much as possible, outside of the general management meetings, where I reported to Geneen and others on the
status of the Defense Space Group. Ned was constantly supportive.

The companies in the group became very strong, and Geneen
placed more and more companies under my direction. By 1974,
close to twenty companies reported to me in the Aerospace, Electronics, Components, and Energy Group, with more than $1 bil-
lion in sales. I had become one of the principal vice presidents and
group executives of the corporation, but still one of more than
thirty.

My group instituted some specific policies and tight controls to
avoid improper payments overseas, at a time when overseas operations of major corporations were plagued with demands by agents
for excessive fees. Through the ITT legal department in Nutley,
New Jersey, our group instituted stiff constraints to be sure that no
problem developed with respect to the use of agents, the payment
of agents, and the actions of agents.

When trouble developed for ITT in connection with sensitive
payments, the ITT companies that served the Department of De-

fense and NASA were never involved. Harold Geneen was extremely proud of the fact that even though other parts of the company had been accused of making sensitive payments, particularly in the telecommunications area, the Defense Space Group was spotless. Nor did this escape the notice of the Board of Directors.

The board had grown increasingly testy about ITT's reputation for integrity. As Harold Geneen approached the age of sixty-five in early 1975, the company's integrity had been called into question, and Geneen's health understandably had been affected. He had gone through a protracted period of great difficulty and incredible personal stress, spending days at a time in Washington with Howard Aibel, the corporate counsel, defending himself and the corporation. There simply was inadequate time to run the sprawling company, and management deteriorated rapidly. But Geneen toiled on without complaint, and seemingly without giving any quarter.

Geneen resisted the importuning of the board for change and finessed their efforts by appointing Lyman Hamilton and me to the Office of the President. It was not that he thought himself irreplaceable, but the double appointment gave him an excuse to remain as referee. He was also under the impression that a couple of last hurrahs would not hurt him or the company, and perhaps the existence of two contenders would allow him a bit more time to accomplish just that.

Prohibited from buying companies with U.S. assets in excess of $100 million, Geneen scoured Europe, and ITT bought up European companies with abandon. Geneen was no longer the critical buyer of yesteryear. In one instance, both Hamilton and I recommended against a potential $15 million French acquisition, but Geneen consummated the deal because one of his European executives had "worked hard" in arranging the matter and deserved a new business.

The European buying did nothing for ITT's position abroad—in fact, it was probably counterproductive. Nor did it help at home: It piled more debt on the company's balance sheet. In addition, ITT's research and development had slowed to a pace that could not keep up with the technology of the digital electronic world. ITT had been a leader in computers, it had been a leader in digital electronics, but it was now falling behind, and, worst of all, did not know it.

My sympathies lay with Harold Geneen. I felt key people had really let him down. He was feeling too alone, too threatened, but, until 1976, I was in no position to help, or to penetrate his own proud barriers. Many key executives feared that we were beginning to witness the unwinding of ITT as a major corporate force.

6

Passing the Torch

Transitions from one business environment to another are always fraught with danger. Companies do not change gears lightly or simply, since habits and traditions—the corporate culture—serve to keep a complex organization on track. Momentum and impetus enhance management, while drag and indecisiveness are the enemies of effective leadership. In the mid-seventies, ITT was floundering: the chairman distracted by Washington political intrigue, research and development uncertain as to direction, and the various power centers of the corporation out of synch. A form of corporate entropy had set in where available energy and useful work seemed to diminish with each day.

At the time, the company was not under siege—the enemy was within. Perhaps it was a form of exhaustion after a decade of rapid, almost unbelievable growth. Finally, after much delay, Harold Geneen was prevailed upon to move, to take a concrete step to revitalize the company.

On the morning of June 8, 1976, I received a phone call at my headquarters in Nutley, New Jersey, telling me to come right in to New York headquarters. Not expecting the call, I was not dressed for the occasion in Geneen's style—black laced shoes, black suit, white shirt, and striped tie. Geneen made it obvious that he noticed my casual attire. (I cleaned up my wardrobe and learned to like black laced shoes.) Later that week, Geneen came over to Nutley with "Tim" Dunleavy and Rich Bennett to Defense Space headquarters, where he had not been for years, to attend a briefing and to confirm to the staff his pleasure that I was moving into the Office of the President.

Ned Gerrity was right in there, in my support. Dunleavy, of course, was beset with disappointment, recognizing that he probably was out of the running and that the competition for the CEO position was between Lyman Hamilton and me. Hamilton was far in the lead. At forty-nine, he was also five years my senior. I knew I was running well back, and it would be a difficult race to win.

The quasi-competition continued, but in February 1977, as I was meeting in my office one morning with Lyman, the curtain descended on my hopes. Lyman was sitting in his shirtsleeves when his secretary walked in with his jacket. A few moments later, word began to swing through the building that he had been selected to replace Harold Geneen as chief executive officer at the end of the year. He would be named president and chief operating officer (COO) immediately. I left my office to see Geneen, stopping to comfort my loyal, red-eyed secretary, Sharon van Hook, who had worked so hard and rooted so earnestly for me.

Harold told me, his eyes glistening, that he had to choose Lyman or the board would have gone outside for his replacement. Board member Felix Rohatyn was quoted as saying Lyman was the only one who was articulate. Someone else had quipped, "Lyman is the only one who can put two sentences together." I thought, What the hell do they know? Jessie was stoical about it. "Hey, Rand," she said, "there's nothing wrong with number two in a $20 billion company."

Holding a number-two position to Lyman Hamilton did not turn out to be that easy, despite the wishes of the board, which had thought we would make a great Mr. Outside–Mr. Inside combination. I was finally elected to the board, but the appointment was a hollow victory.

Geneen stayed on as CEO until December 1977. At his last ITT Worldwide Management Conference at Boca Raton in the spring of 1977, Ned Gerrity produced a movie depicting ITT history under Harold Geneen. In the final scene, Harold Geneen walked toward the camera—only to suddenly pop, alive and dancing, through the screen. It was tremendously effective, greeted by a standing ovation. Sitting next to Lyman, I heard Hamilton mutter to his wife, Mary, "He's trying to make it look like Mickey Mouse could run ITT."

The Geneen/Hamilton relationship soured throughout 1977, and on January 3, 1978, the new CEO announced new policies and a modified reorganization, as if to state, "The King is dead, long live the King." While Lyman fought it constantly, board pressure continued to confirm me clearly as number two at ITT. With no enthusiasm from Lyman, I was named senior executive vice president and chief operating officer, and, most important, a member of the ITT Executive Committee.

Harold Geneen would not give up the chairmanship, so I could not have the president's title. Lyman still held it, together with the chief executive officer position. But making me COO was a positive step. Lyman and I agreed to a working arrangement, with great difficulty, and only after the intrusion of the Executive Committee of outside directors, led by Dick Perkins. At first Lyman wanted me to serve in a staff capacity, but I fought for line control and won it. I also suggested that he not leave Geneen out of key information loops, but he persisted in circumventing the chairman.

The board's confidence in Lyman declined rapidly in the spring of 1979 and dissolved completely by July 11, the day of the board meeting. I was called that morning to meet with all of the outside directors. Tension was high as I was interrogated at great length. Early in the interview, Patrick Lannan, a centimillionaire, chided Fred Hamilton, another centimillionaire, for reading a newspaper while I was responding, saying, "Fred, are you interested in what he has to say?" Fred was not. He had called me over to the Brook Club the night before to ask me how things were going with Ly-

man, and I could only say, "Fred, Lyman is my boss. Ask him."
Something was up.

It was fairly clear that I had broad support on the board. Harold
Geneen was not there. When Felix Rohatyn suddenly said, after
many hours of discussion, "Look, fellows, I've had enough. I'm
in favor of going forward." That was it. Harold then joined us.
The board negotiated with Lyman for his resignation.

That night, at about 7:30, I left my office and encountered Harold Geneen as he was going up to his offices on the fifteenth floor.
He said, "Rand, I am going to Europe tomorrow. There is going
to be a lot of flak."

I figured I could handle it, but I had no idea how much flak
there would be. After the board meeting, I found a message in my
office from Jessie, asking me to bring home some fresh tomatoes.
Excited, I called her with the great news about my new job as
CEO. She said, "Wonderful, Rand, and don't forget the fresh tomatoes!" I hung up in amazement. But that was Jessie. Her excitement was at such a peak that that was all she could say. When
I got out of the car at home, I had forgotten the fresh tomatoes.

The press immediately pounced on Geneen's alleged return to
power and the unfair treatment of Lyman Hamilton. I sent Jack
Hanway, Juan Cappello, and Jim Lester on the company plane to
Brussels to request Gary Andlinger's resignation (Andlinger had
been appointed head of European operations by Hamilton) and to
handle the public relations aspects of the change. I wanted to replace Andlinger with Jack Guilfoyle, a seasoned ITT executive,
and get ITT Europe back under control.

But the newspapers reported that Geneen had gone to Europe to
fire Andlinger, saying it was a continuation of the expression of
his power. Nothing could have been farther from the truth, but
what bothered me most was that we knew that the reporters involved knew it was not the truth.

After replacing the ITT director of personnel, I eliminated all of
the staff product line managers at ITT headquarters, who were
highly paid and producing minuscule results. One of them was

product line manager in charge of skiing, another was in charge of researching food on the *Queen Elizabeth II*. Yet another was charged with seeing how many places in the world he could visit and still be reached by telephone.

I moved to upgrade the technical program, and particularly the leapfrog program for digital equipment known as System 12. I increased the research budget and raised the selling prices on all of the companies ITT was planning to divest: electronic appliances and distributors, drugs, cosmetics, and food companies, principally in Europe. I reduced TV production in Europe from thirteen plants, all over the continent, to two, both in West Germany. I also closed the Rayonier Quebec pulp mill. That was not easy, and it took considerable effort to keep Harold Geneen happy with the decision. It had originally been his pet project. The action caused ITT to have its first quarterly loss since Harold took over in 1959. I sent an eight-person team to Nantucket, where they spent ten hours with the vacationing Geneen, explaining my decision. He never told them his reaction, but he called me the next day. Before he could say anything, I said, "Hal, I couldn't pour all of the ITT you built down that sinkhole in Quebec." He responded, "Rand, I've seen all the numbers. You have to do it." And that was that.

In September, I went to Europe for business-plan reviews of our companies, feeling very much in control. We had lost no one from management whom I did not want to lose. However, there I discovered that Harold Geneen had made plans for investment projects that potentially could become directly competitive with ITT. Immediately on my return, I met with Tom Keesee, one of the senior members of the board and a close friend of Geneen's, and with Dick Perkins, telling them that I would not tolerate this. Harold would have to make a choice—continue as chairman of ITT, with its associated restrictions, or give up the chairmanship and be free to do most of the things he wanted to do. Characteristically, he chose freedom.

Effective January 1, 1980, having just turned forty-eight, I became chairman, president, and chief executive officer of ITT. My first year as chairman was the best financial year in ITT's history—with earnings of $6.20 a share. The System 12 telecommunications digital switching program was looking exceedingly strong, we had already signed a number of contracts, and things were humming.

There were, however, a series of problems on the horizon. The company was about to be hit by extraordinarily high interest rates, plus major expenditures to take people off the payroll in Europe and Latin America. These terminations would cost hundreds of millions of dollars. In addition, as a result of the socialist victory in the 1981 French elections, we were obliged in 1982 to sell our company, Compagnie Générale de Constructions Téléphoniques (CGCT), for a small percentage of what we felt it was worth.

In 1981, nevertheless, performance was respectable, thanks to the results of Hartford Fire Insurance and telecommunications sales in Nigeria. In the fall of 1982, the sale of a significant part of Standard Telephones and Cables (STC) in the United Kingdom produced a substantial capital gain. That gain made 1982 also a successful year financially for ITT, sparking a dividend increase to $2.76 per share in 1982.

It was obvious that the investment community would be looking for further increases in subsequent years. Increasing dividends was a form of orthodoxy, a ritual that Geneen espoused. He felt that the corporation owed it to the stockholders, and he attended to it assiduously.

Trends in dividend payouts over the years have mirrored changes in corporate America. Finance capitalism dictates that the owners of the corporation, the stockholders, put up the money for the enterprise and take the associated risk. Therefore, shareholders were to be rewarded for their risk by dividend payouts that yielded a higher return than that for bondholders, who lent money and assumed very little risk. The yield gap, the difference between what common stock paid and what bonds paid, became a reverse yield gap in the 1960s. Because of heightened interest rates, bonds were yielding more than stocks.

Perhaps it was because of the spectacular rise in common-stock share prices. After all, the rate of return on money was what truly mattered: Whether that came from dividends or appreciation of principal was not of major concern to the investor. In the 1960s and 1970s, high-technology firms and other rapidly growing companies opted to pay minuscule dividends to shareholders—hoping that they would be content with capital gains. Increasingly, corporate management felt pressured to accelerate the rate of growth, whether it was accomplished internally or through acquisitions, so that their common-stock shares would command a higher price in the stock market.

ITT was somewhat old-fashioned when it came to dividends. Numerous pension funds and income investors required or needed dividend income. ITT had high marks from this quarter of the investment community, since the company had raised dividends each year. In the 1960s, ITT's shares soared on growth, then faltered in the early 1970s, all the while continuing to raise dividends. But increasing dividends too much can weaken a company—a fact that was brought home to ITT in the summer of 1984. We were to learn the hard way, in the wrong environment—in the lair of the raiders.

PART II
THE LETTERS

False words are not only evil in themselves,
but they infect the soul with evil.

—Socrates

7

The First Letter

The siege of ITT had started in October 1983, with Jerry Seslowe's approach to Pete Thomas. Although we were not fully aware at the time of the depth and commitment of the raiders' intentions, we were alert to a frontal attack. Corporate Counsel Howard Aibel surveyed the scene and started to prepare our defenses against unfriendly or hostile moves. No one suspected that we would have to defend ourselves from a fifth column, an internal threat. It was not so much a question of naïveté, but of implausibility, since there was no sign of dissension or disharmony after my initial reorganization of top management.

Shortly after a birthday party for Ned Gerrity in January 1984, I received a letter from him at my home in Smoke Rise, New Jersey. It repeated what had been accomplished in that first term and what still needed to be done. What needed to be done, Ned stressed, was the axing of several of the key executives whom I had selected to manage significant activities.

Ned no doubt felt that his long association with ITT (predating even Geneen) gave him special insight into the workings of the corporation. He had spent many years commuting to Washington, immersed in the petty plots and counterplots that passed for lobbying activities in the sixties and seventies. My first impression of him had been formed in 1967, about a year after I had jointed ITT, at a management conference in Washington, D.C. The conference was organized by Ned, calling together all of the ITT line general managers in the United States to see Washington and how it works. As I look back, it was in fact a glorification of Harold Geneen, Ned Gerrity, and the Washington lobbying staff for their contacts and operations. Congressmen, senators, and White House staff members participated in ITT's seminars, speeches, cocktail parties, and dinners. Gerrity, at Geneen's behest, was a top-down lobbyist—never go to the second man when you can go to the first. He had stuck out his neck for the company during the congressional hearings to ascertain ITT's role in Allende's fall in Chile. In fact, he was indicted for perjury, but the case was dismissed. So, in some ways, he felt he had paid his dues, and he probably also felt his advice should now be taken seriously, if not literally.

Ned was particularly negative about Jack Guilfoyle, executive vice president for telecommunications, who had returned to the United States to run ITT telecommunications worldwide after having done a fine job running ITT Europe. Ned insisted that Jack could not handle the job and that he should go. Ned also argued that Cab Woodward was not a decision-maker and could not be entrusted with the financial affairs of the company. He attacked Howard Aibel as dishonest and disruptive, and Pete Thomas as potentially disloyal. He said Herb Knortz, ITT's executive vice president, board member, and comptroller, did not understand the business and in making a speech could clear a room more rapidly than anyone Ned knew. The only person he did not attack at the senior level was Jack Hanway. I read this all incredulously, since nothing that he had written about these executives was true. In fact, I knew it to be all to the contrary.

In the letter Ned stressed that he should be a closer confidant, that we must spend more time together away from the office at lunch discussing the company and what steps needed to be implemented. He explained that I urgently needed his advice and counsel, advice and counsel I was not currently accepting. I reread the letter with dismay.

At the office, I called him in and said, "Ned, basically what do you expect me to do with this letter? Yours is a public relations function at ITT. That is your job. We have not had the best press. Certainly, we have not been treated the way any of us has felt we should have been by the media. There has been little understanding or realization of factors that have affected our company. We received no defense in the media when the French forced the sale of our company. Now, Ned, you have been the man responsible for these activities. I have never criticized you personally for them because I felt that until the bottom line of ITT improves significantly, we are going to be living more with the public relations of the past, and those public relations frequently will be negative.

"Despite all of that, you have taken so much time in this letter to run down everyone in the top management except Jack Hanway. You say that you want to help me more. Well, Ned, you are not the personnel officer for the company."

Ned responded that he simply wanted to be a more significant factor, wanted to advise me more, wanted to be able to get away for lunch more to talk about these things. I said, "Ned, it is pretty hard to go off for lunch with you to talk about people that I have put into significant positions in this company. That is really not my role, nor is it yours."

"All right," he said, "if that is the way you want it." And he huffed off in a characteristic hunched-over walk. Well, so be it, I thought—another maneuver by Ned. That's over with, and now we will go on with business. That was the first letter.

In March I received a call from Felix Rohatyn, friend, former ITT director, and partner in Lazard Frères, ITT's principal investment banking house. He wanted me to know that Harold Geneen had brought Jay Pritzker to meet him. Geneen felt they should know each other because of Jay's interest in leveraged buyouts.

Felix was somewhat puzzled by the matter. After Harold Geneen had left, Pritzker told Felix that he was in partnership with Phil Anschutz and was interested in several companies, including ITT. Felix told him that an attempt to take over ITT for a leveraged buyout would be insane, that the telecommunications part of the corporation would come apart, and that the deal would be spoiled by this likely event. Pritzker said that he was basically interested in something that would bring him a great deal of money in a short period. Felix responded that ITT was not a good answer, but that he would let me know of their conversation.

That again put me on notice, and I subsequently reported the information to the ITT board. I was concerned about the Geneen relationship and asked Howard Aibel to check it out. Harold casually indicated to Howard that Pritzker had wanted to meet Felix, and since, he, Geneen, had had previous financial dealings with Pritzker, he felt it appropriate to make the introductions. "That was all there was to it, nothing sinister." Hal was always quite quick and sure about such matters. He never worried about what others thought, figuring that everyone should be able to look out for himself. If a little introduction could make that much difference, someone was in trouble anyway.

Shortly thereafter, Jessie and I and Ned and Kate Gerrity were off to Rome to attend the formal opening of the Roma, a large ITT Sheraton convention hotel midway between downtown Rome and the Leonardo da Vinci International Airport. It was a tremendous opening, with a fashion show featuring arrogant-acting, leggy models wearing outfits from all of the top Italian designers. The attentive audience included the cardinal of Rome and the Italian ministers of tourism and communications.

The next day, we four were due to fly back to New York. After a morning meeting with the minister of communications, I returned to the hotel to find Ned, Kate, and Jessie waiting for me in the lobby so we could go immediately to the airport. Ned was very pale, and Kate indicated he had not been feeling well. We boarded the company plane and headed home. Ned lay on the sofa most of the way, looking gray. I was very worried about him and suggested that he see a doctor upon his return, which he did. He was told he had to lose some weight and slow down a bit. Ned assured me that he would try to do that, although I knew it would not be easy for him.

It was especially not an easy time to do so, as the ITT 1984 annual meeting was coming up in Dallas, Texas, and Ned and his crew always played a major role. The company had reported disappointing financial results for the first quarter of the year, but we were still optimistic about meeting our financial targets for the entire year. At these meetings, we could generally be upbeat. The audience was positive and the meeting always was relatively short. All of the issues at this meeting were resolved easily, and we returned to New York feeling positive about the state of ITT.

Soon, however, we would be subject to a series of unforeseen and uncontrollable events. While there are always ups and downs in business, within a few weeks we would be buffeted by the arrival of an unexpected storm, one that broke with great fury.

8

The Second Letter

Within three weeks of the 1984 annual meeting, the storm hit. An unexpected metalworkers strike in West Germany began to affect not only all of ITT's automotive and components industries, but also our major telecommunications activities. Predictions by our local German management had been that there would be no strike, but if there was one, that it would be over in a few days. Not so, and the extension of the long strike into our telecommunications area was very difficult for us.

One week later, in late May, the People's Republic of China announced that it was canceling all of its log purchases from Rayonier, causing a $40 million loss for that company in 1984. Then The Hartford's problems of heavy damage claims due to inclement weather worsened. Suddenly, our ability to meet the year's goals was becoming uncertain.

John Pfann, ITT's treasurer, in a memorandum to me reviewing the cash flow and projected cash flow for 1984, recommended that we take steps to stanch the outgoing tide of money. ITT was at that time paying around $450 million per year in dividends. From 1979 through 1984, we had sold off $2 billion worth of companies, but almost all of that revenue had been offset by dividend payments.

Few of those dollars had gone toward improving the ITT balance sheet. In his memo, Pfann had included several possible action plans, including reducing the dividend of $2.76 for ITT's 150 million shares of common stock.

I contemplated the magnitude of what needed to be done. ITT had never reduced its dividend. In fact, dividends had increased every year until the fall of 1983. It had been a difficult decision then, but the dividend increases could not continue. Now the thought of a cut was a wrenching one. Felix Rohatyn had had lunch with Jay Pritzker and concluded that Pritzker was still in the wings. Other raiders were beginning to be active in the Wall Street marketplace, including Carl Icahn, Irwin Jacobs, Ivan Boesky, and Frank Lorenzo.

Mergers and acquisitions, of course, were not new to the marketplace. To work most productively, capitalism requires a reasonably free flow of capital and labor. Conversely, the state is obliged to regulate and control excesses so that the system does not short-circuit itself from an overload of speculative activity and destabilize the economy. Before the raiders appeared on the scene, most mergers and acquisitions were relatively peaceful. ITT, a company with a history of buying companies, never bought one on a hostile basis. It never made sense to buy into problems. But here were a new set of financiers about to unleash a wave of unfriendly acquisitions.

I reasoned that a big cut in our dividend might result in a big drop in our stock: This would cause disappointment among our shareholders and raise the possibility of a completely new set of owners. Yet, if a dividend cut was in the company's long-term interest, it had to be considered expeditiously. The ITT research-and-development program had to be maintained in reasonable order, as did the capital program. We would work hard on reduction of receivables, inventories, staffing, and compensation to reduce costs.

On a hot summery day, June 18, my most trusted senior staff (except Cab Woodward, who was away on a family emergency) gathered in the sun room of my New Jersey home to discuss the enormous implications of my proposal—to recommend to the board of directors a drastic cut in the common-stock dividend from $2.76 to $1.00 per share. There was no time for mistakes, no room for miscalculation.

When I raised the issue with the assembled group, I was met by dead silence and anguished expressions. Even John Pfann, who perhaps best understood the issue, questioned whether such drastic action was needed. While we discussed the impact that a dividend cut might have in the marketplace, particularly if the market over-reacted and did not appreciate the wisdom of what was being done, Ned Gerrity just sat quietly, ashen-faced for a while. Others insisted that the company might lose some institutional backing and sponsorship, and that the credibility accumulated since the political fiascoes of the 1970s would be threatened. Finally, it was suggested that ITT would become vulnerable and that we could lose the company with this one decision.

I struggled with this whole issue—a gut-wrenching experience. Would it be the right thing for the board to do? Was it irresponsible to the ultimate owners of the business to cut their income in the short run? How would the board respond? On that day, the answers were far from clear, but our troubles were evident. The corporation was in a cash squeeze that appeared destined to worsen. Could ITT get through the next year or two and emerge as a vital and innovative company? In mid-June of 1984, these were pressing questions with no sure answers.

We reviewed all of the background facts and then had a lengthy discussion about whether the company's stock would be put into play and what kind of people would become owners. We also anticipated the likely influx of arbitrageurs.

What we did not know was that, simultaneously, Jay Pritzker and Phil Anschutz had begun buying ITT stock at $34 and $35 a share. Before our next board meeting, they would own about 125,000 shares of ITT stock, at an average price of around $32. Two months later, when Jay Pritzker disclosed this to me, I realized that if they had purchased more than 5 percent (7 million shares) of our stock at those price levels before the dividend cut, they would have had no choice but to go after ITT immediately or to take large short-term losses. The timing of our dividend cut was inadvertently opportune for them in the short term, since they were able to acquire a great deal of cheaper stock to offset their earlier purchases. In the long run, their actions were probably favorable to ITT, since their subsequent purchases helped support the price of the shares and also made their total investment in ITT profitable. Clearly, they did not have an urgent financial need to attack.

Staff at our June meeting reached a consensus. They felt that the proposed move was courageous and correct and should be presented to the board. They agreed to support it in every way. Ned Gerrity concurred, but he obviously was uncomfortable. He questioned whether I fully understood the impact of the decision, what would happen. I explained what I felt: The stock could drop to $24, maybe even lower, in the short term, and we could have some serious and unfriendly investors to handle, but if we all stuck together, we could make it, and the company would be the better for it. I reminded them all of the tremendous confidence I was placing in them: Not a word of this could be breathed to anyone.

For the remainder of the meeting, while we discussed the many ramifications of the dividend cut, Ned sat quietly next to Jack Hanway on a sofa, arms crossed, staring straight ahead as though thinking about something else, very deeply. We ended the meeting around three in the afternoon. Everyone was in agreement but realized there would be difficult times ahead. Each departed in a separate car, except for Ned and Jack Hanway, who had arrived together, since they lived nearby in New York's Westchester County. I was concerned about Ned and called Jack Hanway that evening to ask whether Ned had had anything to say on the way home. Jack said, "No, he really didn't. He talked about other things; not about the company; not about the decision. He just seemed very quiet about it, seemed to accept it."

The next day, Jim Gallagher, a tough, young former reporter

who worked in our public relations department under Ned and Juan Cappello, Ned's deputy, called to tell me that the *New York Times* was planning an article on ITT. We had been alerted to it and had been told that the newspaper would want interviews for the article, which would appear sometime in August. I thought to myself that that would be fine. The dividend announcement would have been made, if the board approved it, and any impact should have dissipated. The *Times* article might be critical, but it would appear after the fact and would describe, I hoped, the reasons we had taken this step and, equally important, show a business-type understanding of them.

I then went through the painstaking business of holding a series of private, confidential meetings with the outside directors, starting on a Friday afternoon, June 22, with Michel David-Weill of Lazard Frères at my office in New York. Michel listened carefully and immediately responded in the affirmative. What pleased me most was that he felt it was right to make a big cut; do it once so it would not have to be done again.

That was typical of Michel. He was always clear, concise, and quick. He never second-guessed himself, nor did he worry about himself. When I first met him at his Fifth Avenue apartment, he sat on the couch with his foot up, loafer removed: "The doctor," he said, "thinks I have the gout and said I must watch what I eat." He said it lightly and did not seem particularly concerned. (As it turned out, it was only an insect bite.) His eyes were piercing, his manner courtly. When Michel was angered, the tone of his voice was like the sound of a Beretta being cocked. He always retained a high sense of dignity but did not tolerate fools. Unless asked, he infrequently gave advice. This day, on the matter of the dividend, he was asked, but it was clear that the advice was already on his mind.

Just prior to that meeting with Michel, ITT had been discussing, on a very confidential basis with a Lazard team, the possibility of a merger with Sperry or Unocal. They bore the code names of

Park East and Park West, respectively. We went ahead with the meetings because they had been set up: Work had been done over a period of more than a month, and, of course, no one from Lazard, including Michel at the time, knew about the dividend proposal. A dividend cut would likely make it impossible for us to undertake either transaction in the near term, if at all. So when Michel and I had finished talking about the dividend cut, I indicated that he could appreciate why I had been noncommittal about the briefings the Lazard people had just given to us on Park East and Park West.

He smiled and said, "But, of course, you could not do them if you cut the dividend. I had thought you might do one to avoid cutting the dividend, but I think your way is better. This being so, you have my full support." I then asked Michel if I could quote his full support as ITT's principal investment banker to other members of the board, and he answered, "But for sure."

On Tuesday afternoon, in Washington, D.C., I met with Margita White and Bette Anderson, who had become ITT directors a few years earlier, and explained my proposal to them, asking for their concurrence. Margita White had been high up in the Ford administration, and Bette Anderson had been a senior official in the Treasury Department in the Carter administration. Both of them were strong and firm, and both offered their complete support.

My next visit was to Bob Schoellhorn, a relatively new director, the chairman and chief executive of the very successful Abbott Laboratories. We met at Abbott's headquarters in Chicago. Bob recognized the pitfalls but also the necessity of what I proposed to do, and he voiced his support. I followed this with a breakfast meeting with Terry Sanford, president of Duke University, at the Links Club in New York, and then met with Tom Keesee, Dick Perkins, and Bill Elfers together in my office. All four of those senior directors were in full support.

There was some deep concern, particularly on Dick Perkins's part, that I personally would be in for a rough time. One of my principal supporters, Dick realized this decision would have a major impact and would be tough for me to see through. But he knew there was no other course. He had been an ITT director for more than thirty years, was an avid golfer with an eight handicap, and, at age seventy, was in excellent shape. Dick had been a director while the regal founder Sosthenes Behn was chairman, had worked to bring Harold Geneen to ITT, and had been instrumental in my succeeding Lyman Hamilton. That look of pain in his eyes should have been a warning that I was underestimating what was to come.

The last outside director I talked to was Al Friedman, who had signed on when he was an investment banker with Kuhn Loeb. He had made money on some of Geneen's transactions, particularly the Carbon Coal acquisition. Al had never seemed to be particularly supportive. Near the beginning of my tenure, he had proposed that Darryl Ruttenberg step in with the financial support of Darryl's Madison Fund to take a large stock position in the company to help dismember ITT. At the time, I was incensed. I thought Harold Geneen would have the same reaction, but after the board meeting at which Al brought up the topic, Hal simply said, "Well, that's Al. Don't worry about it."

When I talked to Al, it was on the basis that all of the directors were unanimous in their support of the dividend reduction and that I wanted him to be part of the unanimity. He raised all the obvious questions: about new people owning our stock, the threat to the company, the takeover possibilities, the fact that the stock might drop. I told him that I understood all those things, that Michel had said basically the same things but supported the action. He shrugged his shoulders and said, "Okay, but you are in for it," and hurried out of the office.

On July 10, a new director was slated to be elected at the board meeting—Lawrence Eagleburger, president of Kissinger Associates, former undersecretary of state and former U.S. ambassador to Yugoslavia. I had asked him to come to see me just before the board luncheon at which he would be introduced to the other members. Larry came in and sat down, and I filled him in on one of the most momentous decisions to come before the board of ITT. I explained what I wanted to do and said that he certainly could abstain from voting as a new director, if he chose.

Larry, who knew much more about the company's financial status than most newcomers, because he prepared himself well, immediately responded, "Look, if you had proposed to cut research and development instead of the dividend, I would have abstained. I think companies have to look to the long term. You obviously are doing that. I support that. I want to vote and I will vote with you." I said, "Larry, thank you very much," and we went to join the other directors.

The preceding day, all of the management directors had discussed my proposal to cut the dividend. Herb Knortz felt the cut did not have to be made, that retained earnings were sufficient, but he said he would vote with the board.

These meetings with the directors took place within the context of a growing danger. The afternoon I returned from Washington after speaking with Margita White and Bette Anderson, I had called Ned Gerrity to my office and told him of my dissatisfaction with our overall public relations program, and in particular with our contributions program. I was concerned about the upcoming *New York Times* article; the *Times* had not done a complimentary piece about ITT in years. *Fortune* and *Business Week* were constantly negative and critical and seemed to think that the ITT public relations department tried to manipulate them and tried to control news of ITT. Furthermore, I was not at all happy with our contributions program. We were not managing our contributions to provide the most socially responsible positions or the greatest public returns for ITT. Ned was visibly agitated. I said we should be much more cooperative with the press, allow more access to our management without the presence of the public relations staff, and substantially revamp our contributions program.

It did not occur to me then, but, in retrospect, I should have understood that the ITT contributions program was a power base for anyone occupying Gerrity's position. The date was June 26, and after that, a series of curious events began to break.

On June 28, a return call came from Leslie Wayne to Jim Gallagher, in Gerrity's department. Leslie was the *New York Times* writer assigned to the August story on ITT. Jim asked her what was going on, why had she called Bill Elfers, our director. She told Jim that she had a new deadline—Sunday, July 1. She had wanted some comments from Elfers, but he had indicated he did not comment about a company that he served as a director. He told her he would be happy to talk about his own venture capital company, but not about ITT.

Jim said, "I know. Bill Elfers immediately notified me about the call, and that's why I called you to find out what was going on. Your article was not supposed to appear until August." She replied, "They were going ahead with it right away." She had largely prepared it, and she said she would be glad to talk to the chief executive officer.

Jim indicated that I was then in Florida making a speech to our Abbey Life Insurance salesmen from the United Kingdom at their annual convention in Boca Raton, and that I would be there through Friday. To this Leslie responded that if I wanted to talk with her, it would have to be before Friday afternoon, when she would put the story to bed. Gallagher indicated that this was unfair. As an alternative, she agreed to hold a telephone interview with Cab Woodward on the afternoon of June 29.

The article, which indeed came out on Sunday, July 1, showed a negative sales curve and a generally favorable profit curve for the previous five years—information taken from the ITT annual report. Entitled "The Slumbering Giant," the article was featured with my picture on page 1 of the business section. In it were two quite damaging errors: One paragraph "revealed" that "Rand Araskog had an opportunity to sell ITT Rayonier for a very good price and turned it down." This was absolutely untrue. Second, it said that

"Rand Araskog had refused to be interviewed for the article," which was also untrue.

The article dissected ITT. While it played up a high-life, corporate-style, jet-travel environment for the CEO, it stated that all was not well at the company. The article was disturbing, especially in view of the dividend question under review by the board members.

On July 2, a letter arrived, dated June 27. It went to all outside directors at their homes, and Dick Perkins took his copy to Jack Hanway immediately. Jack called me late that night and said he had a poison-pen letter that was malicious. He knew I would be extremely upset with it, but he did not want to read it over the phone. He felt I should get my own impression of it without any influence from him. But I did ask, "Who do you think wrote it, Jack?" "I don't want to say, Rand," he replied. "I want you to see it."

He arranged to have it sent to my home, and I was stunned as I read this "second letter." The scene had changed; now it said the board had to get rid of Rand Araskog, going into great detail about why this should be done. But what hit the hardest was the last paragraph: "The Board of ITT must take a hard look at what's happening and why. In the end, it will be the Board who takes the blame if disaster hits ITT for it is the Board who decided on the present management and the Board who is turning its back on the problems being caused by mismanagement. You have an obligation to protect the shareholders and employees from possible shallow, face-saving moves that could adversely affect the corporation for years to come. It is time the Board took a hard look at what's happening with our society management and make decisions to stop the slide."

That expression "You have an obligation to protect the shareholders and employees from possible shallow, face-saving moves" obviously came from someone attacking the proposal to cut the dividend, someone who was trying to influence the board against the decision that I would recommend. I got up after reading the letter and walked around and around, in near shock: The style of the letter was just like that of the "first letter."

Howard Aibel and Cab Woodward had seen the letter and were equally convinced of its authorship. I decided I could not live with the continuing suspicion, so on July 9, just before a meeting of the ITT Management Policy Committee, the company's top management committee, I confronted Ned Gerrity in my office, saying, "Ned, do we have a problem?" He asked, "What do you mean?" I said, "Ned, a letter has gone to the board. It's a terrible letter. It attacks me in a most clever and vicious way." Then I added, "It reads just like the letter you sent me earlier this year, although now you have replaced Jack Guilfoyle with me."

Ned was white, perspiring, as he said, "I wouldn't write a letter like that. You know that. How can you think of me that way?" I replied, "Ned, it's the same style; it's the same format. It's the same theme, just the names are changed." Ned looked down, then he looked up at me—nervously, I thought—and said, "Does anyone else think I did it?" I said, "There are three senior outside members of the board who believe it must have been you."

Ned grew more pale, and the perspiration on his forehead had increased. He said, "I can't believe you'd ever think I would. I can't believe anyone would think I would. I love you. I love this corporation."

I waited a long time and then said, "Okay, Ned, let's put it behind us." But, I added, "Ned, it is a real concern to the corporation that a letter like that could be written because it tends to reveal that it comes from very high up and inside our management. Jack Hanway has a copy of the letter for you to read. You can come into the Management Policy Committee late."

He left my office and I walked into the Management Policy Committee meeting. I was astonished to see Ned come right in the other door. Jack Hanway followed a few seconds later. Ned had not bothered to go into Jack's office to see the letter. Jack, who wondered why Ned had not asked to see it, later said, "Rand, to see that letter should have been the most important thing in the world for Ned."

The next day, July 10, Larry Eagleburger and I left my office after our meeting on the dividend cut and went right to the board room, where the Executive Committee of outside directors would carry on an extensive discussion of the dividend reduction proposal. The vote of the entire board was scheduled for after lunch so that Michel David-Weill, who was in London, could be included in a conference vote on the dividend reduction. His strong "aye" came over the ocean just in advance of the other votes, and the motion carried unanimously.

If ITT management on the thirty-third floor had wondered what was delaying the directors' arrival for the board luncheon, they had suddenly had unfortunate excitement in their midst. Ned Gerrity, waiting with the others, had a heart attack. Dr. Jim Wittmer, the medical director, was summoned immediately from the eleventh-floor clinic, and Ned was moved to the clinic to await an ambulance. When the ITT directors arrived, Ned was being taken from the building. I was, of course, extremely shaken.

Ned had been under a doctor's care. I thought back to his illness on the plane on the return from Rome, and Dr. Wittmer gave me some details on his continuing medical problems. When Ned was in the hospital, I gave every assurance to Kate that we would do everything we could to assist her and the family. After the first three crucial days, Ned was recovering well and Kate was in good spirits. Those three days while he lay abed were among the busiest and high pressured of my life.

9

The Third Letter

When the New York market closed at 4 P.M. on Tuesday, July 10, 1984, ITT issued a press release on the dividend reduction. It was picked up by the Pacific Exchange: Our stock was hit immediately and went into a tailspin. There was a fantastic overreaction.

The next day, I was in Minneapolis attending a Dayton Hudson board meeting, but I was in constant touch with Howard Aibel and Cab Woodward. Our stock traded as low as 20⅞, with more than 9 million shares changing hands, knocking the entire market down some forty points and creating a near-record volume on the New York Stock Exchange. At 320 Park, there was fury in some of the phone calls from analysts and investors, large and small. The press was climbing all over our public relations department, run by Juan Cappello, sitting in for the bedridden Ned Gerrity. To me, the overreaction of the market was incredible. Shareholders were dumping stock, which would return to previous levels, at large losses.

I boarded the plane in the early afternoon to return to New York. The flight was terrible, taking seven hours because of thunderstorms all along the route. We were in a holding pattern over Atlanta for two hours before we finally received permission to land in Newark. I arrived home exhausted about 10:45 P.M.

At 11 o'clock, Jessie turned on Cable News Network (CNN), and the first picture was of the New York Stock Exchange with paper all over the floor, and a big ITT symbol. CNN detailed what had occurred—shares that had traded, the way the market had fallen, the total disruption in the marketplace—all of the excitement surrounding ITT. Jessie said, "My God, Rand, you did all of that." I was dismayed, and she said, "Oh, come on, Rand, don't be so serious. I was only kidding. I know it was rough."

A month earlier, ITT had scheduled a TV interview in our offices with the same CNN for Thursday, July 12, at 9 A.M., and since it had been set up well in advance, we felt it would be inappropriate to cancel it. In retrospect, it was good for me to have to stand up to that type of test immediately after the reaction to the dividend cut.

The interview itself was conducted by an engaging Tom Cassidy. The network showed photographs of my parents in Fergus Falls, Minnesota, as well as direct shots of me answering questions. I remember closing the program with a response to a question about how I was feeling after what became a tumultuous step, saying, "There is a lot of heat in the kitchen right now." There certainly was.

The TV program went very well. It clearly portrayed my confidence that we had done the right thing; that we understood, but were not afraid of, the public reaction; that the step that we had taken was necessary for the well-being of the company.

After the television interview, Tom Cassidy mentioned the article in the *New York Times* on July 1 and asked why I had refused to be interviewed. I told him that it upset the ITT board, and that I had explained to the directors that I had not refused to be interviewed; that I had not been given the opportunity. He asked whether I had complained, and I said no.

"Well, you should call Abe Rosenthal and tell him. That should be corrected, because that part of the article really hurt. It confirmed what she wrote. It made it look like you were afraid to respond.''

So after Tom left, I tried to call Rosenthal, but he was en route to the Olympic Games in Los Angeles. His office suggested that I call John Lee, business editor, which I did, telling him about the two errors in the article. I said that we had never had the opportunity to sell Rayonier in the sense of having had an offer. I also said we were working on a possible sale and were probably three months from it when interest rates climbed and the potential deal with MacMillan Blodell fell through. Most important, I told him what I knew about Leslie Wayne's procedures and the fact that I had not had an opportunity to comment or be interviewed, that this had disturbed the ITT board. He offered to put in a retraction, but I said, "No, I just think that would call attention to it." I added, "It was a rough article. I thought I should have had ample opportunity to be interviewed."

John Lee said he would look into the matter nonetheless; that Leslie Wayne was an outstanding reporter and he would talk to her. I wondered whether Ned Gerrity had denied her access to me after feeding her the story. But I only wondered, and then again, I just wanted to forget that kind of conjecture.

The next day was the Hartford Fire Insurance board meeting—a hectic day. Telephone calls were coming in from investment bankers seeking participation with ITT, seeking to help, seeking to defend, offering information, seeking a position. The investment bankers were on the loose, saying that a Pritzker and Anschutz combination was buying in large amounts; that arbitrageurs were buying in all over the place. Names such as Icahn, Boesky, Jacobs, and Steinberg were thrown around at random. We received telephone calls from at least six investment banking houses offering to assist us. The Hartford situation was worsening faster than anyone anticipated. Reserves would be protected, capital gains would be taken, but there was no way of damming the cash outflow.

John Gutfreund, the managing director of Salomon Brothers, called to say he had to talk to me personally. He had important information. He said that large purchases of ITT stock were being made, and there were rumors that the purchasers were people who might be planning to put the stock into play with a takeover in mind. John felt I should do everything to defend the company; not to panic; to take my time and follow the planned schedule. He assured me that the primary interest of Salomon Brothers, as it had been for many years, was to support ITT. I sincerely appreciated his good advice, and I followed it.

Events became wilder on that Friday. I was in and out of the Hartford board meeting all day long. After the meeting, Pete Thomas and I sat down and had a deep conversation about things The Hartford could do to help itself and to help ITT overall—to participate in the defense of the corporation. He seconded the advice of John Gutfreund—stay with the program. I then talked with Howard Aibel and Cab Woodward, and we agreed on a plan of action—Project Blue—to be implemented while I was away in Europe.

To me, Project Blue was born for the purpose of keeping the blue-and-white ITT flag flying over 320 Park Avenue. To Howard, it was "to be prepared for something that came out of the blue." He had established an informal study group a few years earlier to explore the corporation's options should it be subject to an unfriendly takeover attempt. Those early precautions were now about to pay off.

Howard Aibel would lead Project Blue, with charter members being Cab Woodward; Walter Diehl, associate general counsel; John Navin, corporate secretary; Ralph Allen of our beleaguered investor relations department; and Juan Cappello, sitting in until Ned Gerrity returned. Howard would later add, on an ad hoc basis, representatives of outside legal counsel and investment bankers.

That night, I flew to Rome, following a prearranged schedule to meet with high-level Italian officials concerned with ongoing discussions between FACE, ITT's large telecommunications company in Italy, and STET, the state-owned electronics company. STET owned SIP, the Italian telephone operating company. My purpose was to protect the FACE market share in Italian telecommunications. The discussions were cordial and successful, which was fortunate, because I needed a lift.

The eight-hour flight from Hartford to Rome had been difficult. Jessie was with me, and at takeoff we sat together in the front of the airplane cabin. She had read the stories of the storm around ITT, could sense my tension, and asked kindly but somewhat woefully, "Rand, is our life going to change again? Can all this really happen? Can all your hard work go down the drain? What will our life be like?" We talked for over an hour, and I explained what I knew and said that I thought we would be all right. I suggested she get some sleep while I did some work in the back of the cabin to prepare for my meeting in Rome. Distressed by a premonition of failure, I could not work, and I kept mulling over major crises in my life, which Jessie had sensed correctly was also her life.

While in Rome, I received the news that Pritzker and Anschutz were still buying and that millions of shares were trading hands each day. Juan Cappello called to say he had received a call from Jack Anderson, the syndicated newspaper columnist, asking if I was on vacation in Europe. Juan indicated to Jack that I was on business in Italy, then a few days in France, and then on to our Brussels headquarters for ITT's European management meeting. It was very interesting to Juan, and of course to me, that someone had tipped off Jack Anderson that I was in Europe. And, most important, the tipster had erroneously, but perhaps purposefully, indicated that I was on vacation. Juan gave an appropriate response to Anderson's staff, and the columnist did not print that gossip, which made me suspect he did not trust his source.

We went from Rome to Sous-le-Vent, Michel David-Weill's estate at Cap d'Antibes. We reviewed the situation: It was clear that we had a whole new group of investors, that at least 25 million shares of our stock had changed hands. Some of our long-term institutional investors, as a matter of dividend-reduction "get out" policy, pulled out at a low price. I stayed in daily and sometimes hourly touch with Michel and ITT headquarters in New York and Brussels.

On Friday, July 13, I had left Hartford for Europe. Following my departure, letters from shareholders began to come in, largely negative letters concerning the management of ITT, and, particularly, concerning me. The "third letter," dated the day I left for Europe, castigated the Board of Directors: "How could you have done what you did and how could you support a man who headed for vacation right after cutting the dividend?"

It was incredible. I did not know it, but Jack Hanway had concluded, even at the time of the "second letter," that more than one person probably was involved in this. The new letter was briefer but equally devastating. I did not see it until my return from Europe. When I did, I was again stunned. I was no martyr, and I did not relish being burned at the stake.

ITT was about to enter something similar to a war. Arrayed before us was a variety of well-heeled, competent adversaries, and, as we would find out later, the playing field was downhill, in their favor. To make matters worse, and increasing the emotional pressure on me, there apparently was trouble from within.

10

Confrontation

The environment within the ITT headquarters building had changed perceptibly in mid-July 1984. From a relaxed camaraderie among the senior staff people, a note of suspicion had crept into daily encounters. The outside assault on the corporation was almost palpable. Inside, rising tension stemmed from a sense that there was a mole within the organization—a double agent whose motives just might not have been in the best interests of the company. As the summer wore on, a beleaguered mentality settled on 320 Park Avenue—one that was enervating and destructive to all our energies.

We could have circled the wagons, and waited for further erosion of our position. But a defense was not likely to carry the battle. We had to take the fight to the enemy if we were to survive. Part of that strategy was to explain our position to our European colleagues. The trip to Europe allowed me to explain the financial turmoil and clarify our plans.

Throughout the last two weeks of July 1984, I had hourly telephone communications from Europe with the United States, until I returned on July 26. During my last few days in Europe, we held meetings with all of our principal European executives concerning the dividend cut, the effect of the decision, and the strength of ITT. All of the key executives demonstrated a strong sense of loyalty to the company—extremely important because of the powerful position each one held in his own country. I took great personal strength from their positive attitudes and expressions, and returned to New York with renewed confidence.

That confidence helped immeasurably when I walked into the twelfth-floor conference room on July 27 to meet with our investment bankers and the Project Blue team. The tension in the room was electric. The looks on the faces of some of the most powerful people in New York mixed pity with excitement, mourning with anticipation. I smiled broadly at Felix Rohatyn's friendly face and said, "You all look pretty serious." Felix kindly said, "Rand, it's getting very rough out there!"

We reviewed a possible July 31 meeting with the analysts from the financial community. Felix and Jon O'Herron were there from Lazard Frères. It was the first time I had met the Goldman Sachs people—Jim Weinberg, Jeff Boisi, and two or three others. Everyone in the room—including our new counsel from Cravath, Swaine & Moore, Sam Butler, and Alan Stephenson, his partner—was extremely concerned about the company being in play. The purchases that Pritzker and Anschutz had made right up to the day we were meeting cast a heavy spell. Sam Butler did not say so then, but he thought I was a "dead man." Newspapers were heralding the takeover of ITT.

Angry letters were still coming in from shareholders. We operated in a siege environment. In Europe, I had been with our people on the business front lines. Their brand of optimism was not shared by the people in that conference room. Thoughts of dire consequences swirled around in the headquarters tower building in New York. Howard Aibel had set the stage, but now I had to go to the center of that stage.

There was an animated, freewheeling discussion about how to handle the major shareholders—what to do. Clearly, Goldman Sachs was pleased at being added to the team with Lazard. The work that had been done by Howard Aibel, Walter Diehl, John Navin, Cab Woodward, Ralph Allen, and others, while I was away, had been done well. Cab and Ralph Allen had been absorbing the heat from the investment community, and Howard, Walter Diehl, and John Navin had been painstakingly planning the defense of the company with Sam Butler and Alan Stephenson.

ITT's meeting with the analysts took place on July 31. Overall, it went well, considering the situation. Most of the analysts had been with us a long time. I told them we would be reducing executive personnel, that there would be no management bonuses, and that salaries would be frozen. That, perhaps, was what they most wanted to hear. Many of them were to reinstate their buy recommendations.

The meeting resulted in a great deal of press, more agitation about ITT, more interest in the company. The stock had come back up from $20 to around the $24 level. The Project Blue team was convinced that we were nevertheless in for a proxy fight, one that could be launched any day.

At a defensive strategy session with Lazard and Goldman Sachs on how to organize for a proxy fight, Jon O'Herron of Lazard argued for a rising new small proxy house owned and run by one Don Carter, who frequently worked for raiders. Jon said the only time he had been involved in a losing proxy fight was when the Carter Organization was on the other side. Howard Aibel listened carefully to O'Herron and came to me for authorization to consider Carter to lead the proxy organizations we had already retained. Shortly thereafter, Howard and Walter Diehl interviewed Carter and hired him.

Then they brought Carter to see me. He was tall, thin, well dressed, with prematurely graying hair—a preeminently cool character. After talking about his credentials and ITT's problems, he said, "Rand, I've been hired on to keep that ITT flag flying over 320 Park Avenue. I'll earn my fee doing just that. I know the raiders and they know me. I fight rough."

"Don," I countered, "no one is going to get near that flag without one helluva fight. We're very glad you're on our side." The meeting was the beginning of a firm and fast relationship between ITT and the Carter Organization.

ITT's management day at the Conference Center in Bolton, Massachusetts, in early August was well attended. The sunny weather favored the ritual golf and tennis tournaments. Rich Bennett and Jim Lester were retiring, and after the outings we had an honorary dinner for them. Under the circumstances, morale was good and the meeting was upbeat. Our directors were impressed with the high degree of practical professionalism of the ITT executives.

In fact, it was the professionalism and the confidence of the ITT management that set in motion early plans in my mind that perhaps we should take on Jay Pritzker, head-on, before he had an opportunity to take steps that could disrupt the current solidarity of the management of ITT. I was not certain then how to approach Pritzker in a manner that would not seem like a surrender. I began to believe that going directly to his headquarters was the most confident approach, consistent with the confidence of the ITT board and management.

After we had been through our management sessions and board meetings, and after discussion with my colleagues, I made the decision to call Jay Pritzker to confront him about his plans. I told him that I was planning to be in the Midwest and could drop by to see him in Chicago on August 10 if he wished.

He said, "Fine. I'm sorry I hadn't called first, but by all means come on out and we'll meet at our Hyatt Hotel in downtown Chicago and have lunch." We agreed to meet at 12:30.

The tower suite at the Hyatt in downtown Chicago is indeed impressive, as was the ultra-courteous and attractive staff. Jay was not there yet. That day, there was an ITT story in the *New York Times,* which was conveniently placed on a sofa for me to read. Interestingly, there was also a story about Braniff Airlines and the problems that Jay Pritzker was having with his investment. He arrived a little late, and I suspect he was nearby and waiting to give me time to see the articles. He was friendly, with a quiet voice, and youthful for age sixty, as he sat on the sofa, relaxed, in a light tan suit.

"Things have been pretty rough for you, haven't they? You know, we started buying the stock before the dividend cut, but not much, about 130,000 shares. We have an awful lot now. We've got 4.2 million shares, and we're in it to make some money. We're not in it as long-term investors. We think the stock is going to be put in play. We want to enjoy the ride up. Now there are several things I want to cover with you, Rand. First of all, the leveraged buyout matter."

I said, "Absolutely not. You brought that up before. We said no then and we say no now. I gather Seslowe is your man?" He answered, "Yes, Seslowe is my man." I countered, "You are getting bad advice."

He said, "Then how about this? You buy Hyatt from us for up to about 18 percent of your stock, so you don't need shareholder approval—probably about 18 percent would be right. Then you give us some kind of options to buy another 12 percent. In effect, we'll protect you with our 30 percent because you're going to be put in play."

I answered, seriously, "Well, I'll do this. I don't think so much of the idea. I will bring it to the attention of our board and I'll be back to you after our September board meeting, but you must guarantee no more stock purchases." Surprisingly, he agreed. The conversation took place in the course of having hamburgers and colas, and, as I was about to leave, he said, "Say, I'd like you to talk to Phil Anschutz. I'd like to introduce you to him on the phone."

I replied, "That's fine," so he put in the call to Denver. When I got on, I said, "Hello, Phil. I understand your next-door neighbor is Fred Hamilton, a former member of the board of ITT. I was sorry he had to leave our board, but there was conflict of interest over oil holdings."

He said, "Yes, they do live right next door. We are good friends. It's nice to talk to you."

"Look, Phil," I responded, "the next time you are in New York, you are a major shareholder as I understand it from Jay Pritzker, and I would like to see you."

He then asked, "How did your meeting go?"

"I came in here extremely negative. I am approaching neutral. Jay has indicated you are not going to start a proxy battle or create problems but that you are in it to make some money, and I understand that. If someone else starts one, you'd like to join in and make some money on the other side. So, I think we should meet."

That was the end of the conversation, and, despite the invitation, I never met Phil Anschutz until after he had sold his ITT stock more than a year later. In retrospect, the day I had spent with Jay Pritzker at West Point in 1982 probably provided the basis for his agreeing to stop buying shares. No doubt he believed that I would try to work something out with him. He should have kept buying; the odds were entirely with him.

As information developed, some of it conflicting, it seemed that Pritzker and Anschutz, probably in May of 1984, had decided to launch a strategic campaign for ITT. They seemed to be laying the groundwork when the dividend cut caught them so by surprise that it threw off their timing, probably to our benefit.

Early on, Anschutz had tried to tie up Joe Flom, the eminent takeover lawyer, by using his firm on other matters. Unknown to Phil Anschutz, Joe Flom's law firm represented ITT and the Hartford Fire Insurance Company in other matters, thus neutralizing him. Pritzker had Marty Lipton, the "other eminent" takeover counsel, under long-term retainer. In fact, it made little difference, since Howard Aibel chose Sam Butler and Alan Stephenson to represent us.

In our Chicago meeting, Pritzker asserted that Anschutz bought the initial ITT stock and cut him in as a partner afterward. Cab Woodward and I later learned that Anschutz and Pritzker were at First Boston the day after the dividend cut, and that Anschutz was in and out of a meeting, probably buying stock. Pritzker told me he was in Europe at the time and had gotten involved with Anschutz after Anschutz had made some large purchases. Regardless, Jay Pritzker made it clear in our meeting that the two of them were in it together; that they were in it for the short term; and that they did not think I would survive to the next annual meeting. It was a pressure-cooker encounter, one in which Jay Pritzker may have been testing, one in which he was certainly—in his nice, friendly way—threatening. He suggested that he and Cindy have dinner with Jessie and me on their next trip to New York, which only added more steam to the pot. But he did stop buying stock—a major concession. In fact, that visit may have saved ITT.

On reflection, the visit with Pritzker was both the low point and the high point in the war for ITT's soul. Had Pritzker and Anschutz marshaled their forces and acted with alacrity, they might have won. Certainly they had the financial resources to accomplish their goals. But they revealed themselves as too indecisive, too cautious to launch the final assault. With ITT's stock selling in the low 20s, they were not likely to have a more opportune time. They had a chance for the gold ring and missed it.

At the same time, I continued to ponder the motivation of Pritzker and Anschutz. Indeed, I still wonder today about the meaning and logic of wealthy individuals and supposedly responsible institutions undertaking to shuffle the assets of U.S. corporations as if they were playing a card game. Pritzker insisted to me more than once that all he wanted to do was to make a little fast money—as if he were a deprived juvenile. But clearly he did not want to do anything too strenuous to achieve that end. Perhaps he wished to impress his peer group.

I found Pritzker's and Anschutz's activities somewhat demeaning, but no less threatening to ITT for all that.

For the remaining part of August, leading up to our board meetings in September, we watched the stock hourly. Ralph Allen continued to compile letters—almost all negative—from shareholders. We were responding to all of them, putting their names on a list available only to members of Project Blue. Ned Gerrity had returned to work and took the place of Juan Cappello, on the Project Blue team.

The top management team agreed that ITT had to reject all of Pritzker's proposals and keep Anschutz and him away from open combat. Our investment bankers felt that the two did not want public conflict and would hold off. ITT was in its most vulnerable position, its weakest state, and they could have had the company then, but they hesitated and missed the opportunity. It would have been a raging battle. They held the strategic positions. They halted.

On the morning of September 10, I advised the Management Policy Committee, some of whom were members of Project Blue, of my reactions to Pritzker's proposals. I indicated that we had no interest—or at least we were recommending no interest to the board—in the purchase of the Hyatt chain for 18 to 30 percent of ITT stock. Our Sheraton people felt that Hyatt was not doing as well as it had in prior periods. Moreover, legal counsel had clearly indicated that there was no end of antitrust problems between the two hotel chains. So I told the board on September 11 that we had given careful consideration to Pritzker's suggestions and found them completely unacceptable.

The board agreed that Hyatt could not possibly be worth 18 to 30 percent of the stock in ITT and totally rejected the idea as a form of attempted greenmail. And the board was adamant in insisting that ITT remain independent. Larry Eagleburger amused the directors by announcing that he had thought the business world would be boring after his time in the State Department. He said ITT's environment was making the State Department seem like a playground.

The day following the board meeting, I called Jay Pritzker and advised him of the board's decision. He countered by saying, "Well, then, I guess we are free to go ahead with our program."

"Jay, I don't know that I understand completely what that means. I think you are getting bad advice. ITT is a very delicate and

complicated company. I think you'd be sorry to get yourself involved in the wrong way."

And he asked, "By bad advice, you mean from Seslowe?"

"Yes, I mean from Seslowe."

Jay was quiet and then said, "If you won't buy Hyatt, will you
sell Sheraton to me?" He seemed to be backing down. I responded, "No, Sheraton is a basic part of our overall strategy.
Everywhere we have major telecommunications or industrial companies, we have hotels. The fact that we have hotels in Italy assists
us in telecommunications and industrial areas in that country, and
vice versa. Our company is an integrated whole."

Jay rejoined, "I think I understand that." But he added, "Then
if you ever do decide to sell, would you be sure to let us know?"

"Yes, we will," I replied. "We'll keep you in mind." He said,
"Well, all right, thank you." And that ended the conversation.

It seemed clear that Pritzker, for whatever reason—the fact that
Harold Geneen would not cooperate with him, the fact that Salomon Brothers and Lazard were discouraging him, perhaps restrained by Anschutz—was diffidently standing on one foot and
then the other, giving us the time we desperately needed to repair
our fences with old and new investors. We continued to be utterly
vulnerable, ready to fight, but without reserve forces. The quiet on
the front lines prevailed.

Toward the end of September, members of our board and management traveled to Vienna, where we celebrated the one hun-
dredth anniversary of ITT Austria. The press gave great fanfare to
the government's joining in the celebration. The festivities ended
for us at the Vienna Opera House, where we attended a performance of *Der Rosenkavalier*. The cavalier from Chicago was tem-
porarily forgotten, except for constant reminders from Al Friedman
to other board members about ITT's vulnerability. More than once,
I asked him to lighten up.

When we returned to New York, we proceeded through a week
of detailed meetings with Goldman Sachs and Lazard about their

valuation of the company. They also were working on plans for an extended and accelerated divestiture program of about twelve of our industrial technology companies, mostly located in the United States.

During the first week of October, another fortuitous event occurred. I received a call from an investment banker from a small New York brokerage house, who then came to my office to advise me: "The vultures are flying over ITT again." Rumor had it that Pritzker and Anschutz had placed larger orders for additional stock in ITT, beyond the 4.2 million shares that we knew they had. The banker was a personal friend and wondered if he could assist, suggesting some possible combinations with other companies. I thanked him and said that I did not think that was appropriate at this time.

We did some checking and found that a large brokerage firm had probably received orders in very large volume for 100,000 share blocks of stock at up to $26¼ per share—which was very close to our stock price at the time—and that the orders probably came from Pritzker and Anschutz.

On Monday, October 8, a day prior to our board meeting, I called Jay Pritzker. He was vacationing in Barbados, but his Chicago switchboard put me through to him. I told him that an investment banker had advised me that the vultures were flying over ITT, and that those vultures were Pritzker and Anschutz. That was insulting on two counts—insulting for Pritzker and Anschutz to be called vultures, and insulting to ITT to be designated as carrion. I reported that I had insisted to this banker that the rumor was nonsense; that I was a friend of Jay Pritzker's; that there was no indication of any animosity or aggressive takeover interest on his or Phil Anschutz's part. And that ITT was in a strong position as a business, alive and well.

Jay Pritzker immediately said, "I don't know what Phil Anschutz has done." He stammered a little bit. "I didn't think any more stock had been purchased." He indicated they had not attacked ITT management, nor had they expressed disagreement with it; they were simply large stockholders. He reiterated that they were interested in making money, and that they still thought the stock would be put into play, but that they were not going to do it. I said I felt that as a friend I could advise him that we should not be put in the position of having to declare him an unwanted investor. Furthermore, I suggested that he not buy more stock unless he was ready to declare support openly.

I went on: "You told me before that you would not be buying additional stock, and if you are, I think you should let the world know if you really are friendly. Otherwise, I have a board meeting tomorrow. If you are buying more stock now in ITT, I will not carry this charade further, Jay. I am going to let this board know that you are an unfriendly investor and so advise the public."

He insisted, "That is not the case." He seemed to be withdrawing. We talked a bit more, exchanging pleasantries, and then I went back to my meeting. Late that afternoon, we learned that the large orders for additional shares at up to $26¼ probably had been canceled. Whether or not that cancellation was directly related to my call to Jay Pritzker, I did not know, but I believe it was. The next day, we advised our Board of Directors about these developments. They were, of course, excited. We then reviewed our ongoing activities to improve the company's business condition.

We now seemed to have Pritzker and Anschutz off balance. Whatever their game plan, they were not executing it. We probably were benefiting from their compelling desire to be white knights and not black ones. To me there was no difference; to them there apparently was.

Had they managed to strike that fall, ITT might have fallen! What, then, would they have done? There is no telling what kind of precipitous actions they might have undertaken, since they probably had not thought that far ahead. They were clearly willing to join any side in a takeover battle, so there obviously was no loyalty to ITT per se. Undoubtedly, they would have sold off some of the core business to repay banks and others. Since they would have been obliged to liquidate some holdings, ITT would have emerged downsized and decimated. Hyatt would have tried to absorb the Sheraton chain, and the foreign subsidiaries would have been sold off. Indeed, the latter was a ploy still to come, as we shall see.

There are never any exact parallels in the current takeover-raider era, but perhaps the CBS case is instructive. A number of lessons should be appreciated, not only by the public but also by management, boards of directors, and would-be takeover artists. As with most morality tales, the landscape is littered with victims, perhaps proving again that the road to hell sometimes is paved with good intentions. The CBS corporation owned the preeminent broadcast network, with its dedication to excellence in public affairs, news, serious drama, and documentaries. No doubt it reached its zenith under William S. Paley, a gentleman who had a shrewd understanding of the public taste, a keen sense of enlightened programming, and a businessman's appreciation of an income statement. Along with broadcasting, CBS had a famous record division and an extensive publishing arm devoted to magazines and books. When Paley retired in 1980, his third-in-a-row hand-picked successor was Thomas Wyman. Wyman had had no broadcast experience, having been the CEO of Green Giant Corporation and vice chairman of Pillsbury Corporation. He had turned around the troubled Green Giant, and Paley apparently thought he would do likewise for CBS, in the doldrums—in Paley's view, after two successive Paley replacements failed to please him.

Shortly after his appointment, Wyman forced Paley out of the chairmanship and ignored his advice on programming. Faced with mounting pressure from cable systems, independent stations, videocassette recorders, and falling advertising revenue, CBS suffered its first loss as a public company. Diversification into toys and motion pictures did not help. By 1984, the heavy-handed public whipping of General William Westmoreland gave an image of arrogance to CBS. Shortly thereafter, Senator Jesse Helms complained of bias in CBS's news coverage, leading an attack on management by new shareholders. Next, the company was being toyed with by the arbitrageurs, especially Ivan Boesky, as an undervalued situation, trading in the $80 range. CBS's entire independence came under attack when Ted Turner launched an outrageous junk-bond bid, assisted by E. F. Hutton. Turner Broadcasting was already loaded with debt, and it had a net worth of $28.5 million, compared with CBS's $1.5 billion. Turner's paper offering, a no-cash leveraged buyout, was supposed to be worth more than $5 billion, or $175 per share—a great premium over the stock's market price. Instead of giving cash to the stockholders, he offered a package of securities, junk bonds, and some equity. It was novel sucker-bait, but the stockholders did not bite. Wyman also beat back a greenmail attempt by Boesky and went so far as to sue him for financing his tilt at CBS with improper margin borrowing.

Once the company was put into play by Ted Turner, the market price of the stock was manipulated upward. Turner's failure left room for a couple of bids by Marvin Davis, an oil magnate and sometime Hollywood mogul. With more rumors flying and Davis looking for potential partners, CBS stock kept moving upward. Finally, Davis and Prudential Insurance Company reportedly offered Tom Wyman $150 a share for the company on a friendly basis: The price was above the market price but below what Wall Street considered CBS's breakup value. Laurence Tisch had become the largest CBS shareholder and offered himself as a white knight for Wyman. Tisch rejected the idea of Davis's group owning the network.

Wyman had played a lone hand. He did not have the confidence of his board, and when he tried to manipulate them, he began to lose their trust. Furthermore, he had a somewhat detached and lofty leadership style, which did not endear him to employees or shareholders or even some directors. Finally, to fend off the circling sharks, Wyman surrendered to Tisch. Tisch had bought 15 percent of CBS to keep Turner at bay, but CBS, concerned about its independent image, was reluctant to paint him as a white knight. He was welcomed as a "stabilizing influence." Loews, Tisch's organization, finally stabilized its CBS holdings at 25 percent. When Wyman went behind the backs of his two major stockholders, Tisch and Paley, to negotiate a deal with the Coca-Cola Company, his fate was sealed, and the board "reluctantly" fired him and installed Tisch as "interim" CEO.

Thus Larry Tisch acquired control, and soon faced up to the fact that he could not meet the challenges facing CBS without becoming the full-time "permanent" chief executive; although for the sake of Federal Communications Commission doctrine and other legalities, control of the network did not change hands. That, obviously, is a fiction, and Larry Tisch is the architect of "the most subterranean takeover in corporate history, a nontakeover takeover," in the words of *Manhattan, Inc.* magazine. Had there been a formal change of control, CBS might have lost some stations, some contracts with high-priced talent might have terminated, and the shares of the stock could have dropped dramatically. Little wonder that CBS informed the FCC that there was no change in its status.

Yet CBS was forced to pay for its folly with Ted Turner. The company had incurred nearly $1 billion in debt in fighting off Turner, and now faced severe cuts. Within months of the Tisch ascendancy, plans were in the works to cut CBS's work force from 30,000 to 24,000. Even the highly regarded news division felt the ax of the across-the-board personnel cuts. Not long thereafter, CBS sold off its publishing division, and then sold its renowned record division to Sony, the same Japanese company that earlier had purchased full control of a compact-disc manufacturing plant in the United States—also acquired from CBS. Two years after Tisch took over, only the network remains—and it seems dispirited, CBS's famous documentaries a fond memory. Moreover, even with the enormously popular program "Wheel of Fortune," the network quickly slid to third place in the ratings.

The CBS takeover is an example of what might have happened

to ITT. When corporations are targeted, "put into play," and then raided, they are inevitably shorn of their independence, sliced up into component parts, and sold. Even white knights like Larry Tisch have to face up to the debts associated with fending off a hostile offer. Corporations, albeit artificial beings, do develop corporate cultures and esprit de corps. Hostile takeovers and raids, even subterranean ones, cause immeasurable harm and destroy years of continuity. The loss of credibility, experience, and talented people is rarely made up for by the presumed new efficiencies and savings in massive restructuring. Moreover, converting capital assets into cash and Treasury bills, the process of disinvestment, simply for a slightly higher projected return, does nothing for the people who were employed or the goods and services that might have been produced. And in the global game—the only one that really counts—CBS management has helped to make the Japanese winners, Americans the losers.

The CBS affair was still in the future when in the summer of 1984 preparation for something "out of the blue" pervaded our planning. On October 9, on my recommendation, the board elected Ned Gerrity an executive vice president of ITT. He was given that role ostensibly so that he could work more on government matters and prepare Juan Cappello to be his ultimate replacement. In reality, it was a last-ditch effort to save Ned from himself.

Ned was moved to the twelfth-floor executive office, out of his lair on the thirty-third floor at 320 Park Avenue. The move would isolate Ned more from his staff, give Juan a chance to take control of the ITT press relations, and allow us to keep a little better tabs on the media.

The last-ditch attempt at reconciliation did not work; instead, Ned continued to put in a great deal of time helping with a projected *Business Week* article, which turned out to be a cover story. Alice Priest, the principal writer, spent a long time preparing it, with much prebriefing by Ned Gerrity. The article itself portrayed ITT as betting its future on penetrating the U.S. telephone switching market with System 12. The story overdramatized the importance of the U.S. switching market, but that was her theme, and she developed it well.

ITT top management spent the second week of October at the ITT Conference Center at Bolton, Massachusetts, reviewing the company's technology and its future programs. At that time, I felt management was becoming uneasy. Howard Aibel was calm, as usual, but I sensed he was expecting another shoe to drop from some new quarter. It was again too quiet. We all sensed danger. I reflected on the last time I had been at the center, in August, one week following our management meeting, remembering a *Boston Globe* article done by Bob Metz, which was highly critical of the current management of ITT and which Howard and Juan Cappello felt had been planted.

Throughout the summer and early fall, Cab Woodward and I had had constant meetings with First Boston, Morgan Stanley, Salomon Brothers, Merrill Lynch—some of the prominent investment banking houses—in addition to our own Lazard Frères/Goldman Sachs team. This was a strategic move designed to keep them involved and deny their services to hostile raiders. We were, in fact, still powerless in the face of a concerted bid for the company. The price of ITT stock was still down, at about 26; and investors perceived us after the dividend cut as a beached whale with its best days over. Development of our new telephone switching equipment was behind schedule, and there were doubts about its viability in the United States. The raiders, for whatever reasons, had postponed their attack, but a proxy war appeared inevitable and imminent.

11

More Letters

We held a Project Blue meeting in our large ITT conference room on October 17. It was the regular team: Howard Aibel, Walter Diehl, Cab Woodward, Ned Gerrity, John Navin, Juan Cappello, and Jim Gallagher. In the midst of that meeting, Ned Gerrity suddenly announced, "Someone is coming after us!" I asked, "Who?" He answered, "I don't know, but someone is coming after the company."

I asked him, "Who said so?" He responded, "I can't tell, but I heard it at the Westchester Country Club, and I'm sure it is true." I said, "What do you mean you can't tell us who told you?" Ned rejoined, "I promised him I wouldn't say."

We then entered into an incredible, distasteful conversation. I asked, "This is ITT at stake and you refuse to divulge the source of information that could be crucial to us?" He said he was sorry but that was the case.

Everyone was incredulous. Juan Cappello and Jim Gallagher were embarrassed. A few minutes later, the meeting broke up. Shortly afterward, both Cab and Howard came to my office to express their dismay and surprise at Ned's attitude. Cab and I concluded that Pritzker and Anschutz may have found someone to front for them. We had heard the names of Irwin Jacobs and Carl

Icahn, but as yet had no direct evidence of their involvement. I felt that Icahn was too smart to get involved in ITT, that he had other interests.

A little more than a week later, on October 26, the "fourth letter" was posted to the board members. This letter, for the first time, was not anonymous. It contained a signature, "Chauncey Waddell," and enclosed a brief article that had appeared previously in the *New York Post,* attacking not only me, but also Bill Araskog, my son, as an employee of Lazard Frères.

Al Friedman immediately called to express his typical consternation and dismay, since he said Chauncey Waddell was an investment banker. He felt that this letter and the article were very "unfortunate." We soon discovered that Chauncey Waddell was no longer living, but he had had his investment offices at 437 Madison Avenue, where, curiously, ITT maintained offices and our large, top-floor meeting room.

On October 30, an ad appeared on the front page of the *New York Times* noting my fifty-third birthday. At 8:00 A.M., I received a call from Ned Gerrity telling me to be sure to look at that ad, which he and associates in the advertising department had put there. It seemed to be a gesture of friendship. That same night, my son, Bill, told me that Ned had called him that day to tell him not to worry about the *New York Post* article. Bill wondered why Ned had called his attention to the article—he was a bond trader at Lazard, not a merger-and-acquisition man.

We had been expecting shareholder proposals for inclusion in proxy material to be mailed two months prior to the annual meeting scheduled for May of 1985. The deadline for such proposals was November 28, 1984. At the November board meeting, when the "Chauncey Waddell" letter was discussed, we also remarked that the corporation seemed to be sailing into quiet waters. No company-threatening shareholder proposals were slated to be included in our proxy statement.

On November 26, I was scheduled to go to Europe for a week.

I went to the office on Monday morning, prior to my 1:45 P.M. flight. Cab Woodward and I were chatting in his office when Howard Aibel called to say that a shareholder proposal had arrived, calling for the liquidation of ITT. It was a form-letter proposal and had been signed by William Brinker. Because it was a form letter, Howard expected that several other similar letters would follow. Another one came in before I caught my flight. While I was away, three more of the form letters arrived, the last by Federal Express.

All of those letters came from dissident shareholders who were on the Project Blue confidential list. The press had called, or been put up to call, several times to see whether ITT had received liquidation proposals before the deadline. Inquiries came several times that week from the *New York Times*, the *Daily News*, *Wall Street Journal*, and *Fortune*. John Navin and Howard Aibel both thought someone had tipped them off.

On Monday morning, November 26, before any shareholder proposal had been received, Bob Metz, then on Financial News Network, had called me, not the public relations department, about shareholder proposals urging dissolution/liquidation of the company. Did ITT have any comment? Within the hour, the first of the form letters, that from Brinker, arrived. The response to Metz, through Jim Gallagher, was that we were not required to include this proposal in our proxy statement, because it, and the others received later, were technically deficient: The shareholders had not included the statement that they intended to be present at the annual meeting to make the proposal. The other media all had information about the letters before anything was said by ITT.

From the last weekend in November until December 2, Jessie and I were guests of the mayor of West Berlin, where we participated in a series of business and social events. One day, the U.S. commanding general of Berlin let us tour East Berlin in his staff car. We passed through the gates in the Berlin Wall and entered a land of sadness. In East Berlin the children slouched morosely around, a foot-watching-and-dragging lot. A stench came from yellow smoke, telling the tale of brown coal burning in home stoves for heat and cooking. We drove past the bunker where Hitler supposedly committed suicide, toured the famous museum, and drove past the ominous buildings built by the Nazis. I was very uneasy the whole time we were in East Berlin, particularly when we left the car to windowshop.

In 1954–55, I had been an intelligence officer in Detachment R, Office of the Assistant Chief of Staff, Intelligence, U.S. Army. I was in fact with the National Security Agency. After five years of intensive study at Harvard and West Point, I spent a year becoming fluent in Russian. I was assigned to debrief key Soviet defectors at a former Nazi SS camp on the slopes of the Zugspitz in Bavaria. I had been told the KGB had files on me and that I should never go into communist territory. Thus, going through the Iron Curtain, even in the general's car, was not relaxing, and I was relieved when we cleared the last gate and reentered West Berlin.

For a while, I had totally forgotten anonymous letters and shareholder proposals. Late on December 3, we arrived back in the United States—the day another letter was postmarked.

December 4, 1984, was a bad day for Jay Pritzker. He suffered a heart attack and would later undergo heart surgery, putting him out of action for a couple of months. I never wanted that kind of misfortune to befall him, even if it benefited ITT's defenses. I telexed Jay get-well wishes as soon as I learned of the heart attack.

At that time, I did not know that Jay Pritzker's envoy, Jerry Seslowe, had been the originator of all the shareholder letters calling for the liquidation of ITT. Seslowe, Pritzker, and Anschutz had not held ITT's stock long enough, a minimum of one year, to be qualified to submit shareholder proposals themselves.

On that same day, Tuesday, December 4, we had a major break in the psychological warfare against the company. Juan Cappello gave Jack Hanway documents that had been sent to Juan's home on the weekend by Bob Berrellez, a former ITT public relations executive who had been indicted with Ned Gerrity in the Chile affair. Juan had struggled with himself for forty-eight hours before turning over the documents, which implicated senior members of the ITT public relations department in a long-standing plot to destroy the company chairman and, perhaps, to put the company into play.

The documents indicated that Bill McHale, who ran ITT's regional public relations office in Florida, had requested Bob Berrellez, who had recently retired from ITT and lived in Los Angeles, to plant a long article in a West Coast newspaper that was extremely detrimental to the company and the chairman of ITT. It was a highly personal attack, several columns in length.

Bill McHale had lived in Florida for many years. When Harold Geneen first bought a house and Ned Gerrity bought a condominium in Key Biscayne, McHale was always there to maintain communications.

Bob Berrellez, the apparent pawn in all of the Chile accusations, was solicited by Bill McHale to be a pawn again. McHale assured him that the anti-Araskog action was being led by Ned Gerrity. This time, Bob's respect for Ned's deputy, Juan Cappello, and his basic allegiance to ITT kept him from joining the group. So he broke the chain and divulged the information to Juan.

The "fifth letter," signed by a Raymond Case, was mailed on December 3 to the ITT board members from New York. It contained essentially the same information as the press release that Berrellez had refused to plant. At 9 A.M. on Wednesday, December 5, Jack Hanway advised me of the existence of this evidence and showed me the principal documents. Jack had indeed been right that more than one person had been involved. Jack told me he already had investigators and lawyers on the way to the West Coast to interview Berrellez and on the way to Florida to interview McHale.

That same day, I hosted a luncheon for Renato Altissimo, Italian minister of industry, who had once sold ITT a company bearing his father's name. During the pre-luncheon cocktails, Ned Gerrity put his arm around me and said, "It is going to be a good Christmas and a good year, and we are going to do just fine." Deep inside, I shuddered.

Later that same afternoon, at a meeting with several Project Blue members in Cab Woodward's office, Ned indicated he had information that someone was buying heavily into ITT stock with takeover intentions. He provided no background. In view of my previous experience with him, and in addition to the tragic news I now knew, I did not press him for details. In fact, Irwin Jacobs was beginning to move on our stock, but we did not realize it until a Stock Exchange error occurred a day later, Thursday, December 6, and that news became public.

That same morning, Bill McHale was confronted in Florida and refused to talk, but the tape of the damaging press release was still in McHale's IBM typewriter. The evidence was overwhelmingly conclusive, and he was fired for cause. The same day, Ned Gerrity was confronted in his office with the evidence by Jack Hanway and Howard Aibel. He denied any involvement in this activity. Nevertheless, he was suspended as an officer of ITT. Although I was in my office, and Ned knew it, he left 320 Park immediately, and I have not talked to him since. In January 1985 he would formally retire from the corporation.

Perhaps the plot's most revealing evidence was that Jerry Seslowe had solicited proxy proposals through anonymous letters that he sent to a relatively large number of shareholders: All of them had previously written to ITT to complain of the dividend cut, and all of their names were on the secret Project Blue list.

In the rushing tide of events, I had not had much time to reflect on Ned Gerrity's actions. My concern was always somewhat subliminal—I never wanted to believe what I knew. Suddenly a huge incubus was dispelled, and great relief settled over me. Nevertheless, it was a mixed blessing. Gerrity had been my friend, my mentor in my early days with the company. It was he who kept my name and activities within the purview of Harold Geneen. On one hand I felt I owed him, but on the other hand I felt that he owed me and the company more than a modicum of loyalty. When

Ned Gerrity departed, loyalty was not the first word that came to mind to describe his behavior.

That December was probably the most anxious period in the history of ITT, and I felt that the roller coaster would never cease. No sooner had we resolved the McHale/Gerrity problem than we were faced with a powerful new threat.

On Wednesday and Thursday, December 5 and 6, Irwin Jacobs made extensive ITT stock purchases. (He had acquired something of a reputation by salvaging assignments from flood insurers and other damaged goods—hence his nickname, "Irv the liquidator.") At the time, it was far from clear what trouble he could or could not make. His original purchases came to light only because of the mishandling of one of his orders on Thursday, December 6. It occurred to me that Jay Pritzker's absence from an active role could only be fortuitous. I wondered whether Jacobs knew of Pritzker's heart attack. Who could have foreseen the series of events of the week of December 3? It was bizarre, even for ITT.

On Friday morning, December 7, Howard Aibel called the Securities and Exchange Commission (SEC) and indicated that he wanted to brief them on events surrounding ITT. He planned to do it on Monday, December 10. They said no, they wanted to see him that day. In fact, they had been about to call him. So Howard Aibel went down to the SEC and filled them in on everything we knew: the raiders' activities; the anonymous letters; the price swings in the stock; the liquidation proposal; the leaks to the press. It took the SEC a month to digest the incredible tale before it acted.

On Friday, January 11, 1985, the Securities and Exchange Commission began to take depositions, the first from one of the shareholders urged by Jerry Seslowe to submit an ITT liquidation proposal. I inwardly hoped it was the beginning of the unwinding of a network that had threatened serious damage to the company and its shareholders.

Of course, there could have been far more than just an effort to unseat the ITT chairman. The shareholder proposal, if ITT had been forced to include it in the proxy material, would have constituted an easy and inexpensive way for Pritzker, Anschutz—and other investors such as Irwin Jacobs and Jack Stevens of Little Rock, Arkansas—and the arbitrageurs to conduct a proxy battle against the company. If that letter had been in the proxy, we would have had a lot of new short-term investors before the closing date of stock ownership for voting at the annual meeting.

On January 7 and 8, 1985, we held our board meeting at the ITT Research Center in Shelton, Connecticut. During the board's Capital Committee meeting, ITT's divestiture of twelve industrial-products companies was approved, companies with sales totaling more than $700 million, valued by ITT at $300 to $375 million. The board also approved the sale of 50 percent of Abbey Life Insurance Company in the United Kingdom, and of ITT Publishing, Eason Oil Company, and ITT Grinnell, a total package expected to be worth $1.7 billion in cash to ITT.

Our investment bankers had strongly urged a press release on this divestiture program to counter Jacobs's thunderings and the shareholder letters. At first, I resisted, but over the weekend of January 12 and 13, I drafted a release summarizing the divestiture program, scheduled to be completed in eighteen months. The announcement went out on January 16, accidentally coincident with the day Irwin Jacobs began his next charge. The release came as a shock to him, and he lamely remarked that the program was "too little and too late."

General reaction in the business press was very favorable to ITT, and company supporters were ecstatic. There was only one flaw. Goldman Sachs, which had strongly urged such a release, was forgotten in the process and had to read the news in the press. But the affront was assuaged by the deluge of requests the firm received from potential buyers who wanted to look at the large group of companies to be sold.

The whole affair over proxy proposals and shareholders' rights vis-à-vis the corporation raises some burning questions in this wild period of takeovers and corporate restructuring. What are the rights of the people who own the company? Should a company be run solely for their benefit? What is a CEO's responsibility to shareholders? In our instance, the stockholder letters were, if not spurious, certainly solicited for the benefit of the raiders. And the raiders' concern for the welfare of the general stockholders, as for the corporation, was shallow: Their only interest was in making a fast dollar for themselves by dismembering the company.

The successful corporation has many masters in addition to the immediate, sometimes transient stockholders: the government and its agencies; the communities where its plants and factories are located; the employees who work for it; the quality of its products and the level of its services; the charities and public services to which it contributes. The word *responsibility*, after all, is derived from the Latin, *respondere*—to answer to or to be called to account. The successful corporation must be responsible to all its constituents. Shareholder values, to be sure—but not just shareholder values—must be the concern of the CEO. Too much emphasis on the immediate, the short-term, can only be deleterious to the shareholder and the business in the end. Oscar Wilde remarked that a cynic was a man who knew the price of everything and the value of nothing. That definition is remarkably apt for the short-term trader and the raider. To build lasting value, a corporation must be guided by long-term vision.

While we at ITT were aware of the future, our attention that January was riveted on the present. With another raider in the wings, our immediate problem was to survive to fight another day. But the letters would never resume. Our confidence that we could execute our program increased with the removal of those internal mine fields.

PART III

THE RAIDERS

These heroes of finance
are like beads on a string—
when one slips off,
all the rest follow.
—Henrik Ibsen

12

Irwin's Charge

We had done a great deal of research on Irwin Jacobs since December 6. Don Carter, head of our lead proxy firm, had worked for him in earlier takeover attempts and knew him well. If I was proud of my Minnesota farm upbringing, Irwin was equally proud of his father's burlap-bag or gunny-sack collection efforts in the same state. I could even imagine Irwin's father having called on mine in an old truck to pick up gunny sacks.

The record showed that only one CEO had driven off Jacobs. It was not completely clear whether Martin Davis of Gulf + Western had accomplished this feat by a stock repurchase plan (which may have enabled Jacobs to get out with a profit) or whether Davis had called Jacobs from his headquarters in New York after he learned of a large Jacobs purchase of G+W stock, and told Jacobs to get away from Gulf + Western or "he'd be sorry." He quickly got away. I tend to believe the latter, although both incidents could have occurred. Under any circumstances, Jacobs's ball was too much in play to be dropped by ITT.

During the afternoon of January 16, Don Carter came to my office with Howard Aibel to tell me that Irwin Jacobs had just

called him from Minneapolis and had offered him a million dollars
to help Irwin launch a proxy fight against ITT. Jacobs indicated,
according to Carter, that he had gone above the 5 percent level of
stock ownership and would be filing a Schedule 13D, a disclosure
form required by the SEC. Don Carter told Jacobs that the Carter
Organization had already been retained by ITT. Irwin Jacobs repeated the million-dollar offer, Carter refused it, and Jacobs then
stated, "You know this is the end of our relationship."

Carter responded that he understood, but I doubt he believed
any relationship had ended. Jacobs was too practical to carry an
unnecessary and impractical grudge.

The news did increase activity on the twelfth floor and the nine-
teenth floor (the legal department) at 320 Park Avenue. In fact, it
was at fever pitch again. On Thursday, January 17, in the course
of a Project Blue meeting, Howard Aibel was called out to talk to
Sam Butler, our attorney from Cravath, Swaine. Sam indicated that
he had been called by Steve Jacobs, an attorney for Irwin Jacobs,
and that Steve Jacobs had indicated Irwin was interested in buying
certain companies we were selling. When Sam asked whether Jacobs was thinking of paying in cash or in stock, he was told that
Jacobs had no fixed ideas on the subject, that he was prepared to
pay cash but could use stock if that proved to be mutually advan-
tageous. Irwin Jacobs also wanted to know whether we were interested in purchasing back the ITT stock he held. With the
combination of our divestiture program and the sidelined status of
Pritzker and Gerrity, Carter seemed to have moved Jacobs into a
new, more conciliatory attitude.

That same morning, I had been interviewed by *Fortune* magazine and had taken a firm position that ITT would not buy back
stock from any raider, Jacobs included, and that if any one of them
wanted out, he would have to get out in the open market—the same
way he got in.

On Saturday, January 19, Jessie and I went to Washington, D.C.,
to attend some preinaugural parties. In the course of our visit, I

met with Colorado Congressman Tim Wirth, who had responsibilities with respect to the SEC and had introduced a bill that would preclude greenmail. I described ITT's position to the congressman without providing any names of investors, other than those whose names had already appeared in the press (confirmed as shareholders in the company), whose paramount interest was in the breakup of ITT. Congressman Wirth was concerned and took notes, but he offered no suggestions or any indication as to what he might do. He did state that the SEC seemed to be waffling on the takeover issue.

On Monday, January 21, top management had a meeting with Felix Rohatyn to discuss the approach made by Jacobs, and a second meeting on Wednesday, January 23, with Rohatyn and with Jeff Boisi of Goldman Sachs. We concluded that Howard Aibel should call Irwin Jacobs's attorney and let him know that we were not interested in selling companies for stock or buying back the stock. On the other hand, Howard could tell him that our investment bankers would provide him data on a company or companies in ITT that we were prepared to sell. The attorney Howard talked to was a Mr. Lang.

Shortly thereafter, Rohatyn received a call from Lang, who indicated that Irwin Jacobs would like to receive information on O. M. Scott & Sons, our lawn-and-garden company. Rohatyn indicated that a confidentiality agreement would be required, and Lang immediately asked, "What do you mean, a standstill agreement?"

Felix rejoined, "No, of course not. We are not that way; a confidentiality agreement, before you can look at the company." Lang said, "Oh, that will be no problem," and arrangements were made for material on O. M. Scott to be provided to Irwin Jacobs. Steve Jacobs then called Howard Aibel to suggest that perhaps ITT would like to buy Jacobs's holdings of ITT stock according to a complicated formula that would produce proceeds far in excess of market value. Subsequently, Jacobs turned down O. M. Scott.

On Thursday, January 24, a man who would not identify himself—except to say that he was a securities dealer named Flynn—called John Navin, our corporate secretary, to say that Irwin Jacobs had control of 15 percent of ITT stock and had not filed a Schedule 13D. He indicated which brokerage firms held the stock—Jefferies & Company; Stephens & Co; Bear, Stearns; and a small house in New York. He indicated he would stay in touch, but would give us nothing further. Moreover, he remarked that he would be calling only us and not the SEC.

We asked Carter to check out the location of this stock and see whether it was indeed under Jacobs's control. Carter confirmed the presence of the stock exactly as Flynn had placed it in the various brokerage houses. There was no way of being sure that this stock was all under the control of Irwin Jacobs, but it could have been. However, almost ten days had elapsed since Irwin Jacobs had told Don Carter he had gone through 5 percent, and no 13D had been filed with the SEC.

With Pritzker recovering from heart surgery, Jacobs seemed to have launched a last-ditch attempt, perhaps even including "Flynn's" call, to get us to buy him out. Howard Aibel felt the same—that Jacobs did not have enough ITT shares to file a 13D. After all, that would have amounted to 7 million shares, with a value of a quarter of a billion dollars: no small sum for Jacobs to command. But neither had he sold out, nor had the Pritzker/Anschutz interests, so the main battle simply may have been put off for another day. On the other hand, I suspected that Irwin Jacobs had entered into an investment maze far more complicated than he had envisaged in December 1984, when he exploded into our stock, and now he was anxious to get out and to get his friends out with him. Howard Aibel called Steve Jacobs and turned down his stock-buyback proposal.

On January 25, Friday, I returned to Washington, this time to see Bud McFarlane, the national security adviser, to assure him of the condition of the company. We discussed ITT's performance on critical Department of Defense programs, particularly in regard to the hot line to Moscow and the secure telephones used by the

White House and other key agencies in Washington. I assured him that while we might see 13Ds filed, and continued press reports about pressure to liquidate the company, the company was strong enough to withstand attack. Bud expressed his appreciation for the assurance, saying he was convinced that ITT was an instrumental and positive force in the national security communications of the United States. I did indicate that an SEC investigation was under way concerning trading in our stock. He noted that, and that was all. It was a brief but possibly important meeting. McFarlane was in a position to reassure President Reagan if necessary. The ITT-manufactured secure telephone was on the President's bed table, but I am sure he took it pretty much for granted.

I stayed overnight in Washington and had dinner with my daughter, Julie, who was in Washington as part of a Northwestern University master's degree program in broadcast television.

The next evening, I attended the Alfalfa Club dinner with Michael Blumenthal, former secretary of the Treasury under Jimmy Carter and now chairman of the Burroughs Corporation. He had also invited Bill Spoor of Pillsbury and Jim Wolfensohn, an investment adviser from New York. That dinner with Mike Blumenthal signaled the friendly termination of a merger discussion that had begun more than two months earlier between the Burroughs Corporation and ITT. Those discussions had proceeded in parallel with the large Jacobs stock purchases, the shareholder letters, the Pritzker misfortune, and the Gerrity downfall. I could not have handled anything more.

That time period, November 7, 1984, to January 25, 1985, was as intense as had been the period from July 11, 1984, to October 8, 1984. Both carried complex and multiple pressures. ITT hung in the balance in both periods. Without the visceral, psychological, and brainy support of Felix Rohatyn, Michel David-Weill, Sam Butler, the entire board, and Cab Woodward, Howard Aibel, Juan Cappello, and Jessie, I might have pulled the cord on myself—and the company.

13

The Pressure Cooker

Felix Rohatyn had called me on November 7, 1984, saying that Michael Blumenthal, chairman and CEO of Burroughs Corporation, was coming to town and that they would be having breakfast together. Felix felt that ITT and Burroughs might find a mutuality of interests, and he asked whether he could arrange a meeting with Blumenthal to discuss the possibility of some joint activity, up to and including a merger. At that time, Irwin Jacobs was not yet in the picture. Pritzker's heart attack and subsequent bypass operation, together with the SEC investigation of the shareholder letters and Gerrity's retirement, were still over the horizon. Nevertheless, it was still an uncertain time to be talking merger.

IBM had recently acquired Rolm, a major communications-device manufacturer of private automatic branch exchanges (PABXs) in the United States, and since AT&T had aligned with Olivetti, an office equipment company, it was natural to think of ITT having a major association with Burroughs or any other major computer manufacturer. I had already met with Ken Olson of Digital Equipment Corporation in this regard, without reaching any conclusion except that we would continue to pursue some joint programs. There had been meetings with Sperry and Wang to discuss what we might do with them, so certainly Burroughs, which was still very independent in pursuing its own course and had made no alliances, was also a likely prospect. Felix noted that a merger had exciting potential and might also remove the threat of takeover. That, of course, depended entirely on the nature of the deal.

Rohatyn had breakfast with Blumenthal and subsequently called to say that Blumenthal was interested, and a meeting was arranged for 11 A.M. For the first hour, Felix remained with us, as the smooth catalyst, and then he departed. We had lunch and continued to talk, to get to know each other better, and to determine what might be possible. Felix had set the stage beautifully, and we talked Burroughs, ITT, management philosophies, and personal tastes for several hours. We concluded that we would like to meet again in a week to continue the discussions. We both felt a merger of the two corporations could be a positive event.

Aside from the Executive Committee of the board, I decided to limit reports of my talks to Cab Woodward and Howard Aibel. A leak would have been disastrous. Over the years, the ITT Executive Committee of the board, composed of only outside directors, had chafed under the constant leaks, a source of embarrassment to them and the CEO. Leaks had plagued my management at various times—negative plants about Howard Aibel, about company plans, about coming layoffs. It was a game, but a dangerous one.

Mike and I met again on Thursday, November 15, in New York. That discussion ranged through the product lines of the companies, the attitudes of the boards, the specific memberships on the boards, the top managers of each of the companies, and long-term expectations. We did not discuss the matter of who would be the chief executive officer of the new company. I had assumed that Michael would be chairman of the board and of the Executive Committee and that I would be president and chief executive officer.

On December 11, right in the middle of the entire matter with the departure of Gerrity and the involvement of Irwin Jacobs, I told the ITT board that I thought we could consider a merger negotiation with the Burroughs Corporation. The board knew the deal would have to be right for ITT or there would be renewed share-holder disaffection, with catastrophic results for the company. Two days later, I met with Blumenthal again at my offices. At that meeting, I hoped we could resolve the structure of the company and then put our investment bankers to work on a valuation formula for merging.

The biggest apparent problems were the very high Burroughs dividend of $2.80 per share and the cash flow projections of Burroughs and ITT. Although we had begun talks when the sea state was relatively calm for ITT, we were now in the Jacobs storm. While I was under extreme pressure—felt it personally, mentally, and physically—I tried to keep it from showing in our meetings. I kept most of the steam in, but I felt I was inside a pressure cooker.

On December 13, Michael Blumenthal took a completely new line. He began asking about Jacobs and Pritzker. He said that ITT could be saved but Burroughs had to have management control. Because this was all so important to ITT, I labored long and hard with him to try to develop a management scenario that would be acceptable to the ITT Board of Directors, to the ITT management, and, most important, to our shareholders. Sensing this, he became more persistent—insisting that he had to talk with each member of the board before we went forward, that there had to be a clear understanding that he, and only he, would be in charge.

Finally I told him that he was coming on too strong in a way that I did not anticipate. Now I was very uncomfortable with him. I told him I had expected he would want to be chairman of the board, perhaps chairman of the Executive Committee, that I would be president and chief executive officer, and that Paul Stern from Burroughs would head our telecommunications and office products companies, alone a $12 billion combination. Michael would be largely responsible for accomplishing a divestiture program to improve the joint balance sheet, while Paul would integrate the computer and telecommunications activities. I would run the ITT/Burroughs operation.

Mike was insistent that this could not happen. He had to be in complete charge. There was no compromising, there could be no discussion, there was no negotiation. I would be a passive chairman of the board.

Somehow I think I concealed my dismay, saying, "I will be back in touch with you tomorrow. I want to think about this overnight. I want to talk to several of our board members." The board reaction was negative. Furthermore, the management reaction was negative. The board felt that ITT was far too big, complicated, and important a company to turn over total control to Burroughs and Burroughs management. Burroughs was then trading at something like $56 and ITT at $30. On the other hand, the comparable book values of the two companies were 1.3 to 1. The discrepancy in value was too great—ITT's assets were being undervalued. Together with the dividend and cash flow problems, the whole financial structure was such that a deal would be difficult to make, even with complete and singular top-management agreement as to how to accomplish the merger. Perhaps most important, detailed evaluation of Burroughs's strengths and fit with ITT was not looking too favorable.

It was imperative for me to be in constant touch with the Board of Directors, to get its feedback. During my early tenure, I had moved to strengthen the board, enlisting seven CEOs from other corporations. As a result, the board had extraordinary management talent, balanced by four other outside directors from banking, education, and consulting firms to provide an equilibrium.

Corporations can only be as good as their boards. If the mad rush of takeover activity is to be restrained, it behooves the boards of American corporations to apply the brakes. They can, and should, look to what is best for the organic development of the corporation and the interest of all the stockholders.

The decisions of the ITT board on these takeover attempts and merger possibilities were critical for the company. In general, the board believed in standing hard on principle—no greenmail, no

cooperation with raiders. It also believed in maximizing profitability, a decent return on investment, clearing hurdle rates, and conducting a corporation to make it efficient for customers, considerate
of employees, and responsible to suppliers and communities.

Following discussions with members of our board, I indicated
to Mike Blumenthal that we could not continue talking. He was
genuinely surprised, and then wanted me to draw up what was
acceptable. I did so and gave copies to Jeff Boisi at Goldman Sachs
and Felix Rohatyn at Lazard. Over a period of time, I had grown
to know Jeff fairly well. He had worked with Michael before and
felt he could get him to reason with me.

I will never forget a meeting with Jeff when I indicated we were
not going to give bonuses to ITT executives for the coming year;
that, as a result, Cab Woodward's total annual income from ITT
was going to be something like $375,000, and mine would not be
much more. Boisi looked at me with incredulity and sympathy.
This young man, under forty, probably was expecting a check at
the end of the year for between $3 million and $5 million, for
arranging corporate deals. And here was a chief executive officer
of a $20 billion company, one of the largest and most complicated
in the world, who was talking about his chief financial officer getting less than a tenth of that.

However, when Jeff took my description of acceptable terms to
Michael Blumenthal, it did not suit Mike, despite Boisi's appeal
and representations. For some reason, perhaps because of the
Gerrity situation, the Jacobs stock purchases, and the shareholder
letters, Mike had come to conclude that ITT was in distress, that
I was in distress and would accept almost anything. I felt badly
about that. Jeff was urging me to listen to Michael because of the
imminent danger to ITT's survival, but the terms were simply unacceptable.

During the worst of the takeover battle, Jessie and I were never
closer. I was frequently awake at night, and she was awake with
me. I walked and walked in the evening—she was there. She would
come down to the library from our upstairs bedroom and sit with

me. I knew that I had to win the battle, or my life and my family's life would be shattered. I knew that if all was lost, it would affect my son's confidence, as well as that of Julie, who had just moved to the West Coast, and Kathy at Hotchkiss. Perhaps the heaviest burden came when I was pressured by Michael Blumenthal to do something with Burroughs Corporation, and to do it his way—at the same time that we were dealing with the Gerrity, Jacobs, and Pritzker matters.

It was that period that was particularly trying for Jessie, and I loved her so much for enduring it. Kind herself, she always looks first for kindness in those she hopes will be her friends. Life became overbearing for her, and in January 1985, with great wisdom, she decided the best thing for her would be to do something for people she did not know. She was sick of hearing about the greed of raiders, sick of people such as Jay Pritzker and Irwin Jacobs. She went to work at Memorial Sloan-Kettering Cancer Center.

Within weeks, she picked up. More important, it was good for her. Her strength increased, and when she hugged me, energy moved from her to me, powerful energy when I needed it most. She received that energy from cancer patients whom she visited in the hospital. Judith Garden, in charge of the Sloan-Kettering volunteer flower program, became the friend Jessie needed. She was nearly eighty years old, but energetic, consistent, caring, and loving—in other words, kind.

Of course there were light moments for Jessie as well. One night Ross and Laurie Johnson, then of Nabisco and now of RJR Nabisco, invited Jessie and me to join Frank Gifford and the actress Susan Sullivan for dinner. After sharing stories, Susan said to Jessie, with admiration, that she was then playing the role of a wife in a California wine-country takeover situation. "What we have in common," Susan said to Jessie, "is that neither of us knows how our scripts will finally play out." It amused Jessie that Susan, who was playing her television part on a week-to-week basis, didn't know how the drama would end, any more than Jessie did of her real-life situation.

■ ■ ■

Back at 320 Park Avenue, my ITT colleagues were upset by the thought that we might give in to Burroughs. They felt we were far stronger than our investment bankers thought. The casualty insurance business in general was down—it was not just an ITT problem. The highly competitive telecommunications market was not just an ITT problem. The deflation in the natural resources field for a great many companies was not just an ITT problem. So our management reacted to all of this advice by virtually shouting, "Look out, Rand, don't sell ITT or yourself short. We can win on our own!"

I did not sell anything short, but I was becoming impatient with Blumenthal. Fortunately, Felix sensed this, and he wisely suggested that we put all of the Burroughs considerations on hold until after the holidays. The advice was logical for a lot of reasons, the best one being that to try to continue negotiations could lead to a total unfriendly rupture. It was a quiet time for me, a chance to be rejuvenated for more battles ahead.

Unfortunately, a signal changed, and I had to return to New York Christmas night for meetings with Goldman and Lazard to decide whether or not to continue with Burroughs. Soon after the start of the meeting, I stated that the Burroughs discussions were heading downhill. First of all, Burroughs was not coming out well enough in our market and technical evaluation. Furthermore, the pricing that had been discussed at 1.8 to 2 ITT shares for 1 Burroughs share would never sell—not to our board, nor to our shareholders. I insisted that we had to be down around 1.3 or 1.4 shares. This would still be a premium, but the best we could do. At that meeting it was made very clear that ITT was not going to do any deal except a very good one for ITT—and the devil with the raiders.

We discussed the Burroughs developments at the board meeting on January 7 and 8. (It was at that meeting that the divestiture program to sell twelve companies was approved.) We had hired independent technical and marketing consultants to evaluate the combination, and their view was not particularly positive. Most important, I told the board I thought this deal could not be done on a basis acceptable to ITT. They concurred. They also knew ITT was going to be under great pressure—a Schedule 13D might be filed shortly by Jacobs; ITT would be in for a fight. They felt that continuing discussions with Burroughs could not be mixed into that fight.

We advised our investment bankers of our position. Mike and I talked and agreed there was nowhere to go together—except perhaps to the Alfalfa Club dinner on January 26.

Prior to joining Mike for the dinner, I read in the *New York Times* that Jacobs was reported to have made multimillion-share purchases in the stock of the petroleum giant Phillips Petroleum, which was also under pressure from Boone Pickens of Mesa Petroleum in Texas. I thought of the tremendous financial power that Jacobs must have accumulated to be involved in Avco, ITT, Phillips Petroleum, Castle & Cooke, Pioneer, and Tidewater—all at the same time. This man certainly could, with his associates, make a move on the huge fortress of ITT.

I reflected on the incredible leverage that junk bonds had allowed people like Jacobs, avoiding margin requirements. I thought back to the man who had had a reverse kind of leverage and power in the 1960s and early 1970s, Harold S. Geneen. Rumors had persisted that Ken Miller at Merrill Lynch was trying to get Geneen involved in an ITT liquidation effort—on the grounds that he knew the company best, had put it together, and could do the best job of taking it apart.

Harold Geneen had been quoted in *Fortune* magazine as saying that ITT was worth $100 a share, and, of course, with the stock then trading at around $26 a share, the difference was sensational. Salomon Brothers had said our stock was worth $60 to $80 a share on a breakup basis. Other estimates showed ITT, as with many other corporations on the New York Stock Exchange, having liquidation value far in excess of what the stock was trading for.

And breakup was all too conceivable. ITT was fragile due to its

$10 billion of overseas assets. The French had forced the sale of our remaining French telephone equipment manufacturing company, grabbing a property that was evaluated at between $275 million and $375 million for a paltry payment of $32 million. In England, the company was informed, in a gentlemanly fashion, mind you, that it would be nice if ITT sold a majority of its subsidiary, Standard Telephones and Cables (STC). We were given to understand that the future of STC would be in doubt unless we did so. STC was then almost entirely dependent upon British government orders for telecommunications equipment. Brazil was not even polite: They told us to whom to sell our subsidiary, for "one cruzeiro" and an additional amount to be paid out of future dividends, which never materialized. In Spain, officials also threatened the government orders, while burdening the company with enormous social benefit programs for the work force. Thus, the foreign exposure of the telecommunications sector due to legal and extra-legal actions left ITT extremely vulnerable, but really not all that attractive to a knowledgeable liquidator.

Moreover, we knew that telecommunications could not stand alone with System 12 in its late phases of development, that the casualty insurance business should not stand alone in the serious down business cycle. Overall, the company had integrated its investments in research and development, capital, and cash-flow support in ways that defied successful breakup of the company except under the best economic circumstances for its major business interests.

Our press release on January 16, 1985, stating that we would divest $1.7 billion worth of companies (not including Continental Baking, which had just been sold for $500 million) in roughly an eighteen-month period, had caught Jacobs by surprise, and, to a degree, caught the market by surprise. The stock moved up to $33.

At the time, I wondered how that press release must have hit Harold Geneen. Hal would not have been pleased to see ITT absorbed into Burroughs, of that I was certain. With the end of Burroughs merger talks, our fragility and exposure were still of paramount concern. Our investment bankers continually suggested white-knight merger possibilities, while the Board of Directors considered a number of corporate restructuring possibilities to thwart the raiders. Poison-pill warrants, additional debt, and different classes of stock were some of the possibilities to be used in defense, but none of those devices were adopted. Larry Eagleburger commented that since he had joined the ITT board and corporate raiders were running loose, the business community was outdoing the government bureaucracy in the use of colorful euphemisms—mail colored green, shark repellents, and now poison pills.

Two further merger candidates appeared—Wang Laboratories and Sperry. We had long considered an association with Sperry. Dick Bingham—once an employee of Kuhn Loeb, then a partner at Lehman Brothers, Kuhn Loeb, and finally the San Francisco managing partner of Shearson/Lehman—had been a close friend to ITT over the years. So when Dick called to ask if he could speak with Gerry Probst, the chairman and CEO of Sperry, about an ITT-Sperry merger possibility, I agreed.

We met at my apartment on Thursday afternoon, February 21. Dick brought Gerry as well as Vince McLean, Sperry's chief financial officer, and Joe Kroger, its executive vice president for computers. With me were Cab Woodward, Howard Aibel, Bob Smith, and Fred Gibbs. Bob Smith, our senior vice president for corporate development, was a shrewd, tough, and frequently abrasive planner and negotiator. He was also a Jekyll-and-Hyde figure. Socially, he was warm and friendly, with great one-liner humor. In business, he was a bear—snarling, ridiculing, making biting comments and arrogant putdowns. But he was good; he knew what he wanted and usually got it, leaving behind bruised feelings and hurt egos.

Harold Geneen, never known for his tact, once told Bob that he should change his abrasive, unpleasant ways. Bob had the temerity to respond, "Coming from you, Hal, that advice has to be taken seriously."

Fred Gibbs was our computer, communications, technical expert. He had been with the Bell System, spent many years with ITT Telecommunications in Latin America, had run our communications service group, and managed our System 12 development. He knew his stuff and we relied on him for product evaluation and product fit.

We covered a lot of ground—Gerry and I alone in an adjoining room and then with the group in our library. The market price of ITT and Sperry bore a 1 to 1.3 ratio. ITT would be the survivor, I would be chairman and CEO, Probst would head the Executive Committee. When we finished, the Sperry people said they had to go off to see Joe Flom, and I briefed Felix Rohatyn and Michel David-Weill. We had agreed to another meeting the next day, late afternoon, at Dick Bingham's suite at the Helmsley Palace.

Cab, Michel David-Weill, and I attended that meeting with Probst, McLean, and Kroger. Obviously Gerry had been given hard-line and not very practical advice by someone. Suddenly, they were insisting that ITT agree to at least a 2-to-1-share ratio, ITT to Sperry common stock. The companies made a good fit, but we could not agree on the ratios for exchanging shares. The Sperry people thought we were desperate for a deal due to the rumors in the marketplace, so they held out, insisting that Sperry was twice as valuable as ITT. And merger rumors in the marketplace sent Sperry's stock soaring, while depressing the price of ITT. We were vulnerable, but not desperate, so we called off the discussions. I thought it a touch ironic that Sperry and Burroughs merged to form Unisys shortly after our talks ended.

Dr. An Wang of Wang Labs showed great interest in a merger with his company—another excellent fit. He suggested a merger with Wang Labs to be the surviving company. He offered a curious deal, trying to pass off a secondary class of stock that had limited voting powers. Clearly, it would not fly: Trying to introduce a share voting procedure and control from a company owned mainly by one person for an exchange of one class of shares in a widely held public company was virtually impossible. It would have taxed the persuasive powers of Lee Iacocca, and I knew I was no Iacocca at mesmerizing people.

Wang's grandiose proposal included a good deal of camouflage. We did not know it at the time, but his company was in a decline. Shortly after our conversations, Wang reported a precipitous drop in earnings, and his company's shares headed south with a vengeance.

Near the conclusion of these merger explorations, the pressure cooker popped safely, and ITT received a fantastic piece of good news. On March 25, 1985, the SEC had finally ruled on the earlier shareholder liquidation proposals. We would not have to include them in our proxy material for the vote at the annual meeting. Our adversaries now had no free horse to ride. We were elated! The SEC decision, in our view, was 100 percent correct, but we had become leery of decisions by the SEC, which seemed to be becoming more and more favorable to and supportive of hostile takeovers. Still, this most important decision was right, and we were justifiably relieved. But while we may have been out of the pressure cooker, we were still on the stove.

The previous six months had been a period of high anxiety for headquarters management. A whole constellation of problems had been faced and faced down: the dividend cut; the drop in the stock price; the anonymous letters; the mole's activities; the hostile press; the ire of loyal, long-term stockholders; the skepticism of financial analysts; the potential shotgun mergers; the presence of raiders in the wings; and finally the proposals to liquidate the company. Despite the excitement, the cumulative effect had to be debilitating and distracting from the real business of operating ITT.

14

Intrigues

Georges Pebereau, an internationally reputed business-man, came to visit on April 11, 1985. Pebereau, then chairman of Compagnie Générale d'Electricité (CGE), the largest energy and electronics company in France, wished to meet privately before having lunch with me and others on a joint telecommunications project. This discussion was the first of twenty-two meetings between the two of us that would change each of our worlds. It would launch a new international telecommunications group.

At the private meeting, Pebereau told me that an American investment banker had tried to enlist him, together with Wisse Decker of the Dutch Philips, Dr. Karlheinz Kaske of the German Siemens, and Lord Weinstock of the British General Electric Company (GEC), to take over the telecommunications parts of a dismembered ITT in the event of a successful takeover campaign. Georges did not identify the parties involved, but he insisted that they were real, that they had the money and capability, and that they were out searching for people to pick up the telecommunications portion of ITT. He said he had firmly declined to participate.

After Pebereau and his people had left, I talked with Howard

126

Aibel about his disclosure. The idea of the ITT telecommunications breakup technique, the selection of the players, was too clever. I thought it had the markings of a former or current ITT insider working with Jerry Seslowe. Howard and I agreed that I should question Ken Corfield, the managing director of Standard Telephones and Cables, a company 35 percent owned by ITT.

I called Ken Corfield in London and asked him whether he would call Lord Weinstock and find out if Lord Weinstock would tell him which U.S. investment banker was soliciting partners to cut up ITT Telecommunications. I told Ken that I had also called Dr. Kaske, and that he would return my call when he returned from a trip to the Middle East. However, I told Ken I thought Lord Weinstock was the source most likely to assist.

Ken agreed to help, and he called back half an hour later to say that Jerry Seslowe—Ken even spelled the name—had been the individual who had contacted Lord Weinstock to say there were four groups coming together: the Pritzkers were one group; Irwin Jacobs another; a Middle Eastern investment group; and finally a sleeper group. We knew almost certainly that the Middle East investment group did exist. It was headed by an Egyptian who had previously shown interest in buying Sheraton and was a friend of Tom Pritzker, Jay's son. The sleeper could have been someone such as Walt Helmerich of Helmerich and Payne Oil Company, headquartered in Oklahoma. Walt's company had a million shares of ITT stock that had shown no appreciation, but Walt was a stated friend of mine. He would make an ideal popular leader for a takeover attempt or proxy fight.

Lord Weinstock cautioned that this group was potentially dangerous. Ken told him we would make every effort to protect him as the source of this information, but he added that we were in constant communication with the SEC on such matters. The next day, we made all of this information available to the SEC in letter form.

About the same time, Cab Woodward was called by a reporter

in Minneapolis, who had been told by Irwin Jacobs that he, Jacobs, had been served with papers by the SEC asking for his files on ITT. Obviously Jacobs had fed the reporter a good deal of information. The next morning, the *Wall Street Journal* printed an article by Richard Gibson of Minneapolis and Janet Guyon of New York. The article implied that ITT had made some kind of complaint about Jacobs, who stated he was planning to speak at the ITT annual meeting. He said he represented several million shares and was concerned about the direction of the company.

In our view, the offer to speak at the annual meeting was a clever attempt to show the SEC and others how open he was being—a grandstand move that *Fortune* magazine swallowed. *Fortune* agreed to send a reporter if Jacobs would show up to speak. I was not looking forward to hearing more from the "mouth from Minneapolis," but was reconciled to his appearance.

It seemed clear that the two, three, or four groups that Seslowe had told Lord Weinstock about had engaged in extensive discussions about what they might do. At some point, they could decide to come together and file a Schedule 13D. For the moment, they were acting as though the Pritzkers did not agree with Jacobs, except for the fact that they both expressed dissatisfaction, as they said, with the management of the company.

Preparations for the annual meeting were beginning—it probably was going to be newsworthy. The next important date prior to the meeting was Monday, April 22, when Moody's Investors Service would review our bond and commercial paper ratings. Cab felt that if ITT could hold its A rating, we would have taken a major step toward assuring the shareholders about the company's financial health.

Don Carter, our proxy fighter, advised us that he had attended the so-called Pirates Party hosted by Drexel Burnham Lambert at the Beverly Hills Hotel. This annual party for all of the raiders and the junk-bond people had Diana Ross for entertainment and steak and lobster on the menu. There was a special table for the Pritzkers, a special table for Jacobs. Jack Stevens was there; Icahn was there; even Harold Geneen was there. All were out there rallying one another—jokes about ITT by Jacobs; a lot of conversation about a tender offer for another 20 to 30 percent of ITT by the Jacobs and Pritzker group. Carter warned us of this, saying, "It's ninety-five to five that you are going to get a tender offer either before or after your annual meeting for at least another 20 percent of the stock." Carter felt it was likely the offer would occur prior to the annual meeting so they could use the meeting for pushing their program, even though they had lost on their SEC-rejected shareholder proposal.

Then, the SEC's investigation seemed to take on an accelerated pace; the Pritzkers began disavowing Jacobs and Jacobs disavowing the Pritzkers. Seslowe was talking to the newspapers about conversations with ITT. Jacobs was plugging his activities to the press. Obviously, they felt that by putting out information themselves, they could weaken any claim of conspiracy. They received surprising cooperation from the *Wall Street Journal* and the *New York Times* in getting out controlled publicity. But the SEC's investigation was resembling Rip van Winkle in Sleepy Hollow.

On Thursday, April 18, Cab Woodward and I had lunch with Fred Joseph, the chief operating officer of Drexel Burnham, who was about to become its CEO. He was the man basically responsible for establishing Drexel Burnham's near-monopoly at creating junk-bond investments specializing in hostile takeover situations. Drexel Burnham funded all of the major oil mergers initiated by Boone Pickens and had funded most of the hostile takeovers in other industries over the last three years. The firm had developed the junk bond, a high-yielding, low-quality bond that was the currency for the raiders' warfare against corporate America. Among Drexel's stable of a hundred investors were such as Carl Icahn, Ivan Boesky, Irwin Jacobs, Carl Lindner, and Saul Steinberg—people who could be expected to put up seed money in front of the junk bonds.

The Drexel Burnham team, under Mike Milken in Los Angeles,

had put together more than $3 billion from about 140 different investors for the attempted takeover of Unocal by Boone Pickens. Fred Hartley and the Unocal board and management conducted a vigorous defense, only to be convinced by lawyers and investment bankers to follow a scorched-earth policy.

ITT, through the Sheraton Corporation, had commissioned Drexel Burnham several months earlier to develop a creative investment technique for building new hotels. ITT would convert several of its existing hotels into a 40/60 ownership with Drexel Burnham, a partnership that would continue to build new hotels in the United States as ITT's equity in existing hotels was progressively reduced. As a result of Sheraton's relationship with Drexel Burnham, ITT established a relationship with the firm as well.

In addition, the man whose firm owned between 28 and 36 percent of Drexel Burnham, a prominent Belgian, Albert Frere, was negotiating with me for the possible purchase by his Bruxelles Lambert Group of about 25 percent of ITT's Bell Telephone Manufacturing (BTM) in Belgium. Because of this association, of which Fred Joseph was well aware, it seemed very unlikely to us that Drexel Burnham would try to assist any raider in a takeover of ITT. In addition, Joseph had made it clear that they were very careful about not getting involved in situations where they felt there would be negative public reaction or a negative result. For example, he indicated they had turned down participation in any takeover effort against CBS.

Lazard Frères and Goldman Sachs were certain that only Drexel Burnham could raise the kind of money required for a takeover attempt at ITT. They believed that Drexel Burnham could put together as much as $6 billion in a single package. Cab, Howard, and I felt that they would not get involved. Much of our strategic information—such as our evaluation of potential moves by investment bankers other than our own—we shared only with one another.

During the meeting with Joseph, I had an opportunity to convey a couple of messages to the Pritzkers and to Jacobs, if Joseph chose to pass along those messages. They were messages of the strength of our resolve. Joseph said he thought it was interesting that Anschutz had not come to see me, and he also noted that he believed these fellows felt it very difficult to get out when they were in a loss position. I responded, "That's true of any investor, but Pritzker and Anschutz are not in a loss position."

The upshot of the meeting was that Drexel Burnham and Fred Joseph would prefer to have a normal financing and banking business with ITT rather than be involved in the junk-bond financing of a raider attempt to take the company. ITT had covered all of the major investment banking houses and was doing business with all of them.

During our meeting with Moody's on ITT's debt ratings, we were grilled rigorously. We had to be well prepared—and were. My adrenaline was running particularly high in the two-hour presentation that I gave as lead-off speaker. Following me were Pete Thomas; Edmund M. Carpenter, executive vice president for industrial technology; and Cab Woodward. We made our points that with the actions we were taking—reduction of debt, sale of some companies—we were healthy financially. The Moody's people were far more friendly at the end of the meeting than previously. It was also clear that, prior to the meeting, they had all but made a decision to downgrade our ratings.

The meeting lasted for almost six hours and included their top people. Perhaps the most beneficial aspect of the session was a subsequent clarification that under no circumstances would they revise our rating prior to our annual meeting, only three weeks away. This was not out of kindness; they simply did not have enough time to complete the evaluation, to do additional evaluations at The Hartford, and to interview certain of our System 12 customers before making their final decision.

In another critical step to shore up our defenses, we touched base with all of our important bankers. Cab and I met with Walter

Shipley at Chemical Bank to reaffirm our relationship. Shipley made a strong statement that Chemical's board and management had adopted a firm policy not to participate in the financing of an unfriendly takeover of a client company.

ITT had significant banking relationships with Chase Manhattan, Manufacturers Hanover, Citibank, Chemical, Bankers Trust, Bank of New York, BankAmerica, Morgan Guaranty, and Irving Trust, as well as banks throughout Europe from Midland Bank in England to Deutsche Bank in the Federal Republic of Germany. We counted on our strong long-term relationships to help ensure that these banks would not support a raider organization against ITT.

Prior to our annual meeting, I spent a day in Minneapolis at a Dayton Hudson board meeting and a day with my parents in Fergus Falls, Minnesota. My father was approaching eighty-four and my mother eighty-two, and I was concerned that a major confrontation before or after ITT's annual meeting might worry them needlessly. So I went to reassure them, to let them know that come what may, I had had a very successful and happy life, a good career, and had no regrets.

We went to dinner at a restaurant overlooking the large, deep, and very blue Otter Tail Lake, a spot where I had spent many happy summers. After a get-together with other members of the family, I left Fergus Falls with a feeling that seeing my parents had been the right thing to do at that time.

The annual meeting on May 15, in Savannah, Georgia, of course featured the perpetual corporate gadflies, Evelyn Y. Davis and Lewis Gilbert, plus Irwin Jacobs. We later found out that two representatives were there for Pritzker and Anschutz, as well as reporters from much of the business press.

Prior to the meeting, we had a "family" dinner with the ITT directors and the Helmerichs and the Weinmanns. The latter two families had sold us Eason Oil, and each had a million shares of our stock. They had joined us in years past for these director dinners. In the course of the evening, Walt Helmerich paid particular attention to all of the directors and the discussions. Walt had told me earlier in the day that he had been contacted on frequent occasions by people purportedly representing Jacobs and Pritzker to get him to lead a move against ITT. Walt would not do that, he said, because of his confidence in the company and because of his friendship with me.

That evening I told Walt I had just learned that Pritzker and Anschutz had voted their stock against management. It originally had been voted by their broker/representatives with management, but they were now changing their votes. Their vote would be fairly obvious because the vast majority, something like 116 million out of 128 million shares accounted for, were being cast for management. I told Walt I felt they were being foolish, but so be it—the fat was in the fire.

At the annual meeting, Irwin Jacobs was sitting in about the tenth row with his attorney. Evelyn Y. Davis and Lewis Gilbert were seated right across from him. I gave a fairly long "state of the union" message, and then Gilbert and Davis traded tracks to the microphones. Jacobs obviously was getting antsy. Suddenly, he jumped up to grab a microphone, but Mrs. Davis got there at the same time and said, "Ladies first." Irwin shrugged and sat down, and I remarked, "Mr. Jacobs, now you know what I have to put up with." The room exploded in laughter, and I knew then I had him—and so did his lawyer.

Lewis Gilbert attacked Jacobs as a poor manager. I had never before appreciated Gilbert's and Davis's presence at annual meetings, but now they acted like my picadores. Jacobs finally bulled up to the microphone, said he would probably need more than the allotted five minutes, but hoped he would be forgiven. He plodded, sometimes losing his place, through a long, handwritten speech. When he finally sat down, I thought I saw two ITT managers—absentmindedly, I hope—applauding.

Jacobs got nowhere. Later, he tried to become argumentative, but I heard his lawyer tell him to sit down. He turned and snarled at him that he was going to make his point. He never did.

The ITT board felt that Jacobs's statements were not particularly well delivered. To them, he seemed nervous and agitated and finally had to wander off to trivial matters about whether or not I had made certain statements to *Business Week,* the character of the statement, and the time of the statement—all rather pointless.

In response to a question from Evelyn Y. Davis as to whether Pritzker and Anschutz had asked for greenmail, I responded, "No comment." Their representatives were in the audience. I remembered Jay's 1984 offer of Hyatt Hotels for 18 percent of ITT and options for 12 percent more. At the time, it certainly seemed like a form of greenmail.

Near the end of the balloting, Howard Aibel informed me that the Pritzker/Anschutz votes were being changed in favor of management. I thought that startling, but knew nothing more about it at the time. The final count showed an overwhelming majority for management: 116 million out of 128 million votes, one of the largest responses by our shareholders, with about 88 percent of the shares voted.

Afterward, directors and management had a luncheon. Walt Helmerich told me that he had stepped out of the annual meeting to call Jay Pritzker to tell Jay that he was making a mistake, that he would be standing alone, that the board was united, management was united—that he ought to vote with management. Walt told me that Pritzker had told him that he would talk to Anschutz; they apparently had two or three telephone conversations. Pritzker told Helmerich he was having trouble with Anschutz. Anschutz did not want to vote with the company. Finally, Pritzker said he convinced him to vote with the company, and they began their vote changes.

All of the vote changes apparently did not arrive before the deadline. At the time, I told Walt, "I appreciate what you did, but I certainly hope they don't feel there is any obligation on our part, because frankly, I don't care how they voted because of the overwhelming vote we had in our favor. The only thing I wouldn't have liked was the negative publicity.'' Walt Helmerich said he understood, he called them entirely on his own, because he felt they were making a mistake, that there was no reason for Pritzker/Anschutz to be in opposition, since it was an ineffective negative vote.

We then went to our board meetings. There seemed to be genuine appreciation and excitement on the part of the board for the way the annual meeting had been conducted.

The flight home was a pleasant one. Jessie, of course, had been at the annual meeting and had watched carefully; she was in the best of spirits, feeling that it had gone extremely well.

The press reports of the annual meeting were generally accurate, but still significantly overplayed the efforts of Jacobs in constructing a platform for a takeover attempt of ITT. Jacobs apparently came to our annual meeting principally to act in the open, and also because he had an agreement with *Fortune* to be there and to speak. The magazine was doing a profile on him, and he must have felt they put the heat on him to be there. So ended the high drama of the ITT annual meeting of 1985 in Savannah, Georgia. ITT was coming out fighting—and now on the offensive.

15

The Counterattack

Jay Pritzker, Walt Helmerich informed me, was extremely upset. Pritzker had learned from his representatives at our annual meeting that I had responded, "No comment," to Evelyn Y. Davis on the question of whether or not Pritzker and Anschutz had attempted to greenmail ITT. Walt said he tried to explain to Pritzker that this was just an answer to get rid of the question, but Pritzker was adamant. They were insulted and wanted an apology. I indicated to Walt that I had been told by our attorneys that I should respond to any question regarding greenmail with "No comment." I went on to explain the whole background of the Pritzker/Anschutz relationship, including their original attempt to get us involved in a leveraged buyout, as well as their efforts to presell our telecommunications companies in Europe.

Seemingly shocked and dismayed, Walt said he would call Pritzker to tell him he had no interest in pursuing the matter further. Pritzker had asked him to come to see me with Anschutz to make an offer for ITT. He said he planned to tell him that that was purposeless and that he would not join in. I thought that was well advised, and I appreciated his position and his call.

Shortly thereafter, Walt called again, saying Pritzker was not satisfied. Walt thought he was ready to quit hounding ITT but needed to be satisfied. Pritzker still felt insulted and Walt was attempting to mediate: "Rand, I think you should call him."

I said, "Well, if you feel that is a good idea, I will check with my legal counsel, and if they say okay, I will do so. In general, I'm averse to the idea."

Howard Aibel talked to Sam Butler at Cravath. They agreed that I should call Pritzker on this issue, so I did. I told him that I was calling to thank him for changing his vote, that I felt he had done the right thing. He went on to tell me that they had only done it because of Walt Helmerich's call and their belief that his call was at my request. I made it clear that Walt did it entirely on his own and I was pleased he had done it, but ITT did not request the vote change. Pritzker sounded somewhat taken aback by my aggressive attitude. He went on to make some indirect offers, such as saying that Hyatt people could be helpful with ITT telecommunications in Indonesia. I explained that since ITT had been in Indonesia a long time, we knew our way around pretty well, but that we would never refuse assistance if it was proper and effective. Then came the grabber. In a very low, whispered voice, which he adopted on these special occasions, he said, "We'd like to come in and talk to you about an offer for the company."

I replied, "Fine, but as I said at the annual meeting, it will have to be for a full price. And remember, it will have to treat all shareholders equally. By the way, don't come in with that price [$38 to $40] you tried to get Helmerich to join you with. That won't even begin to fly."

Pritzker responded that he would have to think about what to do, then went on to discuss the "greenmail insult."

I countered, "I answered that question that way to be rid of the subject matter. I am surprised that you would expect an apology from me, in view of the activities of Seslowe with his attempts to get an improperly solicited letter into our proxy material, a shareholder proposal calling for liquidation of the company. Then consider the fact that Seslowe has also been running around Europe trying to find buyers for parts of ITT. You're a major shareholder of this company, supposedly one of the most responsible of business people, how could you authorize and allow your name to be used in that fashion? You expect an apology from me? You've got to be crazy!''

Pritzker was completely taken aback. He alleged he was unaware of the shareholder proposal and the letters until after they were reported in the press. He admitted, however, that he was aware of Seslowe's efforts to peddle parts of ITT around Europe.

Finally, I said, "If you and Anschutz wish to see me, you come right ahead. I will be glad to talk to you."

"I think we've talked enough," he said. "Thank you very much and good-bye."

Not long after that call, an article appeared in the *New York Times* quoting Pritzker sources as saying, "Pritzker was still very displeased with the performance of the company, with the management; felt it was moving too slowly, that he had had discussions with Rand Araskog and that Rand Araskog had been completely taken aback by the fact that Pritzker was still interested in a buyout of the company." It was a very pro-Pritzker article, entitled "ITT's Future Seems Unclear." I was irritated that the *Times* continued to print these planted stories without checking with me or others at ITT as to the reliability of the information or soliciting our response.

I sent Walt Helmerich a clipping of the article, along with a note saying that perhaps now he would understand the people he was dealing with and for whom he was carrying messages.

After the annual meeting, we had a major restructuring of ITT. Two vice chairmen were appointed: one for all corporate mergers and acquisitions and financial developments, Cab Woodward; one to run our service companies (Hartford, ITT Finance, Communications Operations and Information Services, Sheraton), Pete Thomas. A new president and chief operating officer, Edmund Carpenter, would be responsible for the manufacturing companies, which included industrial technology, natural resources, and telecommunications.

Soon there were more stirrings from Pritzker. I received a call from Harry Gray, chairman and CEO of United Technologies, indicating that he had been contacted by the Pritzker group and offered $25 million if he would lead a takeover of ITT. He said they already had the financing, were ready to go forward, and had buyers for the various pieces of the company. He wanted me to know that he had turned them down. I expressed my appreciation and told Harry that we had been going through these sorts of shenanigans for several months.

He then told me not to relax. The raiders had told him they planned to go after Bill Johnson of IC Industries or Don Kelly of Northwest Industries to replace me. Gray was expected to step down as CEO of United Technologies at the end of 1985, and, I suppose, they felt he would be the best person to carry their colors.

We soon learned they apparently had also tried to enlist Walter Wriston, formerly of Citicorp; Dick Shinn, formerly of Metropolitan Life Insurance; Sandy Weill, formerly of American Express; Alexander Haig; and other prominent businessmen for a blue-ribbon board, but they had struck out, despite offering potential board members a large share of the spoils.

I called Howard Aibel's attention to the heavy "corporate establishment" content of those being sought, not only to replace me but also to constitute the board. They seemed to have become concerned about appearances, especially in official circles. After all, ITT operated in more than eighty countries, and many of their governments were our most important customers.

With investment bankers scrambling to try to divide up the spoils of major American corporations and heap debt—heavy debt—where equity currently resided, it was hard to blame commercial bankers for wanting to get in on the action. As Fred Hartley of Unocal so aptly put it, "We are replacing the warm blood of equity with the cold water of debt."

American corporations could have stopped, or at least reduced, the destruction of the takeover business if they had united early in the game and presented a common front. A number of steps should

have been followed—the first of which would have been to drop
the services of investment bankers who supported hostile takeovers. American business should have put greater pressure on the
government to halt some of the takeover mania, a plague that has
caused loss of many jobs, closing of plants, and decimation of
small, one-industry communities. But the Business Roundtable, an
organization of two hundred large corporations, could not get together on it. Moreover, Washington was infiltrated by investment
bankers—Donald Regan in the Treasury Department and then the
White House, John Shad at the SEC, and other key figures in the
Treasury, State, and Justice departments. The revolving door between these agencies and the Wall Street houses leaves the clear
impression that between campaign contributions by investment
banking and the high pay awaiting former officials not much will
be done until after another cataclysmic crash in the markets.

The wheel has come full circle: Even the commercial banks now
compete for a piece of the profits from the takeover game by providing loans for leveraged buyouts. The commercial banks all ral-
lied around each other when Saul Steinberg first went after
Chemical Bank. At the time, Steinberg's attempt was stymied by
overwhelming support for Chemical from President Nixon, as well
as from Nelson and David Rockefeller and the money-center banks.
Today, irony of ironies, Chemical is one of the chief lenders in the
merger-and-acquisitions business. Whether or not commercial
banks should be in this business is an interesting question. What
happens when all that highly leveraged loan paper can no longer
be serviced in the next recession? Will leveraged-buyout loans join
the Third World loans? Commercial banks, above all, should realize the danger of leveraging up America. Former SEC commis-
sioner John Shad made eloquent speeches about this subject, but
he never did anything concrete to stop it.

The last week in September, I was in Italy as the guest of the
Agnellis and other members of the Atlantic Bridge, a setting in

which CEOs from both sides of the Atlantic discussed international trade between the United States and Europe. We were joined by government representatives from the United Kingdom, West Germany, France, and the United States. Telecommunications obviously was regarded as a target of opportunity by European and U.S. Government officials, and ITT's market share was the bull's-eye. I was appalled at the American trade representatives' lack of knowledge about American companies. They were supporting AT&T against another American company, ITT—to the obvious glee of our European competitors, who could only benefit by the U.S. representatives' ineptitude. The European companies had the best chance at getting some of ITT's market shares, so why not let the American trade representatives stir the pot?

Several days after the trade conference, I was in Paris for meetings with former Prime Minister Raymond Barre; with Edith Cresson, the minister of industry and trade; with Georges Pebereau and Jacques Dondoux, the head of the Postes, Téléphone, Télégraph (PTT). In a meeting at the Elysée Palace, I was assured by Alain Boublil, assistant to President François Mitterrand for telecommunications affairs, that ITT was most acceptable again in France and would receive favorable consideration for business relationships developed with CGE. So the road seemed quite clear ahead for more specific discussions with Georges Pebereau and our dream of the future.

In October, the ITT board approved certain resolutions related to change of control in order to protect ITT's officers' options, previously granted. We also committed the excess assets in our pension fund to medical benefits for retired employees. The steps received a small amount of publicity as antitakeover-type efforts, which they were not. They were steps to protect employees' rights, but employee rights are largely forgotten in press accounts of takeover activities.

Prior to the October board meeting, an article had appeared in the *New York Times* suggesting that Jay Pritzker had made efforts to solicit a blue-ribbon board for a takeover of ITT. This spurred us to unlimber the big guns, since shareholder proposal time was again approaching.

On Friday, October 11, after considerable discussion with both the board and its Legal Affairs Committee, ITT filed suit in the New York courts against Jerry Seslowe for his shareholder liquidation proposal activities and for other efforts to manipulate our stock. The suit, of course, provoked a big reaction. We had detailed the suit some months earlier, but updated it with recent statements made in a *Times* column that contained more vintage Seslowe.

The suit set ITT on an entirely new course. The company was on the offensive and counterattacking. We would seek discovery of Pritzker's and Anschutz's records and files. Seslowe had verified each of them as principals in a letter to Richard Dieterich, one of the shareholders who had been solicited in the fall of 1984. We had turned that letter over to the SEC. We secured the assignment of the case to Dave Boies, Cravath's top trial lawyer, and we were ready for deadly serious combat.

In Washington for a meeting with President Reagan and the National Security Telecommunication Advisory Committee (NSTAC), I emphasized ITT's strength and independence before traveling to Horseshoe Bay in Texas to speak to a conference of Southwestern Bell's senior managers. My message was simple: "ITT's telecommunications products are the best available, Southwestern Bell is one of our most important customers, and ITT will remain an independent corporation." Their managers, who had never been subjected to the takeover game, were fascinated by my report of what had been happening at ITT.

Shortly thereafter, on October 12, a *Fortune* article included Jay Pritzker's picture and indicated that he had been attempting to put together a blue-ribbon board to replace ITT's board, that he had also contacted several people through Jerry Seslowe to see if they would lead the efforts to take over ITT. The article indicated that Pritzker had not been successful. However, the article also quoted

Irwin Jacobs as saying that he was sick of the whole lot of us at ITT, which did not upset any of us too much. Shortly after that article appeared in *Fortune*, Jacobs called to request a meeting with Cab Woodward on Thursday, October 17. He wanted to talk to Cab because he had seen him before and felt there was no point in talking to me, but he never showed up for the meeting.

In any case, Cab did not want to meet with him—Cab told me it was my turn. After Jacobs's only meeting with Cab and Bob Smith in March, before the 1985 annual meeting, Jacobs had later said that he "had met ITT management and they're a bunch of dummies." Bob Smith did not care, but Cab was rather sensitive about that.

16

The Raiders Retreat

The war of nerves intensified in mid-October 1985. Mobilization had led to skirmishes, which exploded into open hostilities. The lawsuit filed against Jerry Seslowe had brought things to a head. We learned that *Fortune* magazine was doing yet another major piece on ITT, based on Pritzker's efforts to assemble a new board. It appeared we were in for an extremely critical article—anti-ITT, antimanagement, and anti-ITT's board. It would probe the whole relationship of Anschutz, Pritzker, and Jacobs, plus their intentions toward ITT. I could tell that Howard was concerned, and that, of course, bothered me.

An analyst with Goldman Sachs informed us that he had been called by *Fortune*. He said they were doing an extensive article that looked as if it would castigate ITT and its board for failure to negotiate with Pritzker. I decided to call Pritzker to alert him to the article. I felt he should know that neither of us would like it. He had been giving a consistent "no comment" to press inquiries while letting Jerry Seslowe do the singing, but Seslowe had given too much information to the magazine and created too many erroneous background details to justify a "no comment" from either ITT or Pritzker now.

Pritzker, however, felt the article was developing the way he wished, and he told me he would continue with his "no comment." He did confirm that at one time he had thought the board should be replaced (apparently including his good friend Terry Sanford), but he no longer felt that way. Pritzker was friendly and conciliatory, which made me all the more wary of what *Fortune* was about to do.

Throughout the week, we worked a great deal with the magazine reporter, who obviously had talked with a number of ITT-haters and disgruntled former employees. Juan Cappello and Jim Gallagher were doing a thorough job of getting our positions on the record with *Fortune*.

We briefed all our directors on the *Fortune* story, except for Ralph Davidson, the chairman of Time Inc., whom I did not feel it would be fair to notify, since Time Inc. owned *Fortune*. The magazine was reviewing its final details with us and finally got through to Pritzker. They told him they were going ahead without his comments, but that the piece had a good deal of coverage of him and he should take this last opportunity to talk with them. After hearing some of what *Fortune* had prepared, he thought better of his previous stance: He had a two-hour telephone conversation with the editor. Much of the conversation was a conference call, with both Seslowe and Pritzker on the line. We were informed that after that conversation Pritzker was far more upset than we were, and he let it be known in language the editor would not repeat.

No doubt Pritzker warned Phil Anschutz about the forthcoming story. Anschutz probably had had enough of the ITT caper when the lawsuit was filed against Jerry Seslowe. If not, the news about the article probably sealed the doom of the Pritzker/Anschutz cooperation on ITT investments. Pritzker had about 2.3 million shares and Anschutz a little over 2 million shares. Apparently they separated in late October, and Anschutz began selling his stock in the $33 to $35 price range, for a nice gain, since his purchases with Pritzker had been at an average of about $23.50 per share.

This was also a time of decision for Irwin Jacobs. Should he stay in the stock and do battle? He told Myron Magnet, lead writer on the *Fortune* article, about ITT's top managers: "I've had it up to my neck with them. Those guys are the biggest bunch of losers I ever met." Cab Woodward was right to be sensitive. He had never said anything unkind about Jacobs's bankrupt snow-blower business.

In any event, Jacobs sounded as though he was ready to surrender to the "losers." He and his group had purchased their 4.3 million shares—of which he had 1.1 million—for about $32 per share. They had held it a year at high interest rates and needed a price above $34 per share to break even. The stock was then at $32. It seemed unlikely they could make any kind of a tender offer because of the huge financing requirement. The Seslowe lawsuit filed by ITT probably made Jacobs (not directly involved in the suit) nervous as well.

As part of our planned counterattack, we were asking injunctive relief and large damages. Among the charges were violations of the securities acts, improper proxy solicitation, insider trading, market manipulation of ITT stock, and improperly attempting to force the company to liquidate itself. We further charged that ITT had been put into play to reap enormous financial benefits at the expense of ITT, its shareholders, and the investing public.

Indeed, Jacobs had much to be nervous about. Seslowe was nothing more than a messenger boy—small potatoes. Was the suit an omen of other litigation to follow? Jacobs's record was scrutinized, since he and his controlled corporations had been accused repeatedly of violating federal statutes and regulations. The Federal Reserve System had accused him of submitting false and misleading information in connection with a proposed stock-redemption plan involving Mid-America Bancorporation. In fact, he paid $50,000 in civil penalties, the largest penalty ever assessed by the Fed up to that time. His proxy solicitations in the contest for Pabst Brewing Company had been challenged successfully in the courts as misleading.

Whether the Seslowe lawsuit, and the possibility of others, decided the issue is unknown, but there were signs that all the raiders might be getting out. After some discussion with Cab, I called Fred Joseph, head of Drexel Burnham Lambert, to see whether he could come to my office to talk with us. I planned to suggest to Joseph that he contact Jacobs, for whom he had done a good deal of business, and simply tell him that in his judgment it was time for him to get out of ITT stock if he was still antagonistic.

Fred courteously came by to meet with Cab and me, but he indicated it was impossible for Jacobs to get out. He would have to be taken out, because Jacobs would be unwilling to lose money. Joseph added that if Jacobs sold, everyone would know. Only through Bear, Stearns could the sales be kept secret for more than thirty seconds. This was news to me. They had come into the stock quietly except for a trading error. I assumed they could go out the same way—quietly.

We discussed ways to buy back the stock with no greenmail implications, and ended agreeing to talk with Fred again the next day. There seemed to be no way to accomplish a buyback in any practical fashion, but the thought of having Jacobs and Pritzker around for another year was enough to keep me searching for trapdoors—for them.

On Tuesday, October 29, before we could do anything more with Drexel Burnham, we heard a rumor that "Irv the liquidator" was liquidating; that he had already sold 2 million shares through Bear, Stearns to an international account (subsequently identified as Soros, a major money-management firm). Jacobs then had about 500,000 shares left, but the word was he was getting out entirely. We also heard that Phil Anschutz had reduced his position substantially and might also have as few as 500,000 shares remaining. We felt that perhaps Pritzker had not sold in order to avoid looking afraid of the suit that had been filed against Seslowe, his financial adviser.

On Wednesday, October 30, there was a great deal of selling. In fact, during that week and the closing days of the previous week, nearly 10 million shares of ITT stock changed hands. We knew that Jacobs's Minneapolis friends and Jack Stevens of Little Rock held about 4.3 million shares, and, of course, that others might be selling. It seemed clear enough, in any case, that Jacobs was selling. On October 31, rumors spread that this was indeed happening. On Friday, November 1, around the close of the market, Jacobs announced that he had sold out all of his ITT stock and had no further financial interest in the company. There was a mixture of relief and disappointment for me, but I quickly overcame the feelings of disappointment.

The following week, I called Fred Joseph and said I didn't know whether any mental telepathy was involved, but that Jacobs had done the right thing in getting out at the levels he had, rather than staying in to fight a battle I was sure he would lose. Fred felt it was also good for ITT, saying, "If there was any mental telepathy involved, it was yours, not mine."

I replied, "Whatever, we are now in a different situation and I just wanted you to know that we appreciate your willingness to sit down and discuss the entire matter with us and to consider how to handle it."

We at ITT were gratified to see the stock holding up in the $34 to $36 area. We heard that another purchaser, money manager Fred Alger, had bought 1 million shares. We also learned that Walt Helmerich had sold his million shares.

The issue of *Fortune* carrying the article on ITT ("Is ITT Fighting Shadows or Raiders?") was dated November 11, but it came out a week or so earlier. In the large volume of trading in ITT in late October, we suspected Pritzker might be selling too. By the time the article was published, all were gone. Myron Magnet closed his story with "Seslowe says Pritzker is now waiting to see what Irwin Jacobs, who has been rattling his sword loudly, will do. At ITT hearts are still pounding."

Who could know? Perhaps, it was the imminent magazine article—combined with the lawsuit against Seslowe and the adamant position of our managers and board—that caused other hearts to pound as they ran away from ITT.

On Thursday, November 7, the *Washington Post* published an article specifying the size and importance of the SEC investigation into stock manipulation and insider trading. It quoted Garry Lynch, the SEC's chief of enforcement, to the effect that the commission was extremely concerned about these activities, but also concerned that the SEC would have difficulty proving wrongdoing against particular people.

After their November 11 article, *Fortune* called ITT to ask about the Pritzker and Anschutz holdings. We simply referred them to Pritzker and Anschutz. Seslowe had told *Fortune* that Pritzker had sold no stock and had bought no stock in many months, and that Anschutz was still a major shareholder. From everything we knew, this was not true. We only told the magazine that Pritzker had informed us he had no intention of making any hostile move against the company.

The ITT board had every reason to be proud of its consistency. The *New York Times,* in an article on Monday, November 11, was quite candid, blaming the cannibalization of Revlon by Pantry Pride and Ronald Perelman on the Board of Directors of Revlon. That board's willingness to auction off big pieces of the company after a leveraged buyout tender led by its chairman, Michel Bergerac, led to Perelman's obtaining control with a higher bid.

I felt that the strategy that ITT had stuck to religiously—holding the company together, defending the company, not being willing to spin off desirable assets, not being willing to auction off pieces that were basic to the core strategies of the company—was correct.

In a free-market economy, individuals and corporations should be free to buy and sell companies if our resources are to be put to their best and most effective use. However, the major consideration for many of these takeovers has more to do with self-fulfilling prophecies of some egomaniacal financiers and overweening ambition of some investment houses than with business and productive efficiencies.

Too many deals are being done because of the ability to do them—not because they have any sound economic logic or business validity. Admittedly, the subsequent arbitrage activity in a takeover target does raise the price of the company's shares in the market-place. This "surfacing of value," as it has been called, has helped some stockholders realize the real or underlying value of their shares.

But at what price to the target company? If it is a "friendly" takeover, the only way to accomplish it—without using one's own money—is by issuing junk bonds, using the assets of the target corporation as collateral. Thus, junk bonds have been called "the rocket fuel of corporate raiders," who are naturally reluctant to use their own funds. If it is an "unfriendly" attempt, the corporation may manage to defend itself and fight off the unwanted suitor by selling off assets and/or taking on substantial debt, which debilitates it further. Or, if it is unsuccessful in its own defense, the corporation becomes the "cash cow" to pay off the junk bonds used to vanquish it. Either way, the company is saddled with debts that not only weaken its finances but also jeopardize it during a business downturn. Furthermore, should the target company be acquired, it may well be dismembered and its parts sold off to help pay the acquirer's bills.

What makes pirate raids possible is this use of junk bonds—low-quality, high-interest obligations. Some institutions—such as banks, insurance companies, and pension funds, which should be in the forefront in the fight for a stable business environment—line up to buy junk bonds in order to raise their yields on their bond portfolios. But, in doing so, they lose sight of their obligation as fiduciaries to invest, and not just speculate with, their clients' funds. Their heavy participation in this area was brought home sharply after the October 1987 meltdown, when the markets for junk bonds evaporated faster than spilled tea on a hot stove. Even though the markets subsequently revived, many were hurt, deep into deep pockets. Shallow pockets collapsed.

What should the federal government do to level the playing field? The Federal Reserve took one step by ruling that investors in leveraged buyouts must obey margin regulations that require investors to put up at least 50 percent of a stock purchase. This ruling was designed to stop raiders from financing a takeover with notes issued by an intermediary shell company set up solely for the acquisition.

But that has not stopped the game. More needs to be done. In my estimation, the regulatory agencies and Congress should consider a number of additional measures that would slow down the torrent of takeovers:

- In order to curb rampant speculation in potential takeover candidates, require that an acquirer have all financing in hand before the public offering.
- Eliminate, reduce, or restrict the use of so-called highly confident letters issued by investment banking houses. We can be highly confident that the sun will rise tomorrow, but financial promises are on a different order of magnitude. "Highly confident" is largely in the eye of the beholder.
- To forestall rushed or panic actions, extend the duration of the tender offer from twenty days to sixty or ninety days. This would give stockholders more time for a considered judgment.
- Outlaw greenmail and golden parachutes. This would put necessary starch into the backbones of wavering boards and would preclude payments by crony boards of directors.
- Shorten disclosure time, when an acquirer has taken a 5 percent position in a company's stock, from ten days to one day. This would reduce the risk of underhanded or sneak attacks. Or even consider reducing the 5 percent rule to 1 or 2 percent.

- Rigorously enforce the regulations against "parking" stock—keeping shares in a third-party name to avoid disclosure.
- Mandate that an offer for more than 10 percent of a company's stock must be made to all shareholders.
- Finally, consider altering the rights of stockholders. By giving long-term investors (those holding their shares for at least one year) exclusive power to vote on stockholder proposals, the destiny of the corporation would not be placed in jeopardy and at the mercy of arbitrageurs and speculators. A one-year ownership requirement for voting would calm the troubled waters of corporate governance without depriving the true owners of the means for ousting incompetent or unresponsive management.

It is important not to make a blanket indictment of mergers and acquisitions: Some are clearly healthy and inject an entrepreneurial vitality. Not every corporation is a model of efficiency, productivity, and business acumen. Some deserve to be shaken up. On the other hand, the work of earlier raiders, such as James Ling, Meshulam Riklis, and Victor Posner, is hardly inspiring. Nor is the work of some present-day raiders—T. Boone Pickens, Asher Edelman, and Irwin Jacobs, not to mention Jay Pritzker.

In addition, there is a role for the states to play to reduce some of the abuses. Obviously we need national markets, but states have a responsibility to their local communities and local shareholders. A number of states—such as New York, Massachusetts, Minnesota, and, most recently, Delaware—have passed laws to regulate unfriendly bids that would dismantle, strip, or destroy regional companies for the perceived financial benefits of some distant corporate monopoly players. Corporations must make their views known to their state legislators. If they await Washington's actions, they are likely to have solutions dominated by the thinking of investment bankers and their Wall Street law firms. In this takeover era, game plans from that quarter are sure to be antithetical and unsympathetic to corporate needs.

If some of these suggestions were enacted, stockholders, corporations, and the public interest would be better served. Besides injecting a sense of equity into what has thus far been a one-way street, they would reduce the rate of debt in the nation (the country now has just about all the indebtedness it can stand, more than is good for sound financial health) and would help further stabilize the financial markets. The wild volatility of the early and mid-eighties—some of it directly attributable to all these mergers and acquisitions—would cease. Exorbitant debt and volatility can never be compatible with business and financial stability.

It is entirely possible that we have passed the crest in raider-inspired takeovers. Certainly the Delaware takeover statute, signed in February 1988 (one that T. Boone Pickens adamantly opposed), is constructive. Delaware is the home of nearly half of the companies traded on the New York Stock Exchange and more than half of the Fortune 500 industrial companies. The new law is likely to put a major crimp in junk bond–financed offers by making it more difficult for a raider to sell or borrow against a target company's assets and squeeze out minority shareholders. However, the new law will not negatively affect fully financed offers for 100 percent of a target company. As long as many companies are perceived to be undervalued by the market, however, it is too much to expect that there will soon be a complete halt in the takeover mania.

It is somewhat ironic that the SEC—which many observers feel has been less than energetic during the 1980s in enforcing laws and regulations entrusted to its jurisdiction—promptly and with great bursts of enthusiasm took issue with the Delaware takeover statute and laws of similar ilk enacted in other states. Also, it is interesting that the first constitutional challenge to the new Delaware law was made by BNS, Inc., a joint venture of sorts of the British Beazer group and Shearson Lehman Hutton Holdings Inc. (a subsidiary of American Express Company), which had commenced a hostile tender offer for Koppers Co., Inc., an old-line Pittsburgh industrial company. Notwithstanding its eventual success in this raid, American Express no doubt had second thoughts about its inappropriate role in a hostile takeover when Pittsburgh residents were shown on national television cutting up their American Express cards. Local citizens could only envision another empty business complex, à la the Gulf Oil Corporation tower.

There is another reason to suspect that we may have passed the crest in hostile takeovers. Public shareholders are beginning to recognize that companies run by the takeover artists are not only no improvement over professional management, they are frequently worse. The Texas Air complex of Frank Lorenzo is a case in point. Eastern and Continental airlines are in worse shape—whether judged by profits, efficiency and timeliness of flights, maintenance, safety margins, or enforcement of regulatory orders. Carl Icahn has TWA leveraged up to its eyeballs with long-term liabilities nine times greater than the common equity. Moreover, the raiders are no bargains for stockholders when the target company does manage to defend itself, since it inevitably takes on heavy debt to ward off the attacker. Unocal and Southland are two examples in which the raiders not only did not enhance stockholder values, they depreciated them. Of course, some corporate boards, such as those at Gillette and Goodyear, have only themselves to blame for paying greenmail.

Happily, corporate raiders of late have barks worse than their bites. The situation was best summed up by Professor Warren Law of Harvard Business School, who remarked that "Most raiders haven't had the problem of demonstrating what they can do with major companies because they haven't acquired them." He suggests that if they did, they would not know what to do with them. "It would be like the (barking) dog that eventually caught the car."

At ITT, with the raiders finally gone, the war of nerves was over and we could again turn our attention to building the company on a sound financial basis—and I did have a plan, whose code name became Roxane.

PART IV
ROXANE

Some women'll stay in a man's memory
if they once walked down a street.
                    —Rudyard Kipling

17

The Ravishing Roxane

With the exodus of the raiders, we had to get down to serious strategic work. The health of ITT was still far from optimal in the fall of 1985. Our debt servicing remained a burden, and long-term debt still was more than a third of the company's capitalization—too high. Our cash position had improved, but not yet in any dramatic way. We continued to sell off companies that no longer fitted with our business plans. This helped to sharpen the focus of ITT as a multinational service and technology corporation. Nevertheless, our exposure to foreign pressures and politics left us uncomfortable, liable to attack or other unpleasant surprises. I was determined to reduce that exposure, and perhaps turn our foreign assets into a fortuitous advantage. A joint venture appeared most likely to lead us out of our dilemma.

If we could sell our European telecommunications manufacturing facilities to a strong European telecommunications company, or possibly establish a new entity, we could reduce our foreign liabilities while bringing in substantial funds to improve our balance sheet. That would be an elegant solution to a complex problem.

Over the years, it had become apparent that ITT's telecommunications facilities were in a bind—one that was likely to get worse, not better. There were a number of reasons for the current cul-de-sac—some political, some technical, some financial—all detrimental to ITT's health. In many nations, telephone service was regarded as a quasi-state monopoly, rather like the mail and telegraph services. Furthermore, the manufacturing of telephone and switching equipment was regarded as a national patrimony, highly regulated with slow, measured technological change. The swelling of nationalist sentiment around the world led to pressure on almost all of our subsidiaries to buy them out, force them to sell at absurdly low prices, or accept joint partners on highly disadvantageous terms. The writing was on the wall in the 1970s and early 1980s.

Another element was the looming computerization and digitizing of telephonic networks. New systems were bound to make obsolete some of the capability of electromechanical systems. ITT's plants were likely to suffer in any national competitive strategy. Moreover, we also began to envision alliances of major electronic companies—AT&T and Philips, Siemens and GTE, GEC and Plessey. The competitive strength of these international combinations could be awesome indeed.

Keeping the system up to date was inevitably expensive, and costs could be recaptured only by attracting new customers. Designing software was also expensive. The need for cash, whether obtained through a joint venture or through government sponsorship, was great. But while the United States had deregulated its telephone system with the AT&T consent decree, other countries were nowhere near so hospitable to foreign producers and products. Deregulation might well come, but the lack of accessible markets was yet another reason for finding a joint domestic partner in these countries.

In short, there were a number of formidable reasons to seek an alliance if ITT was to be rid of some of the problems inherent in being considered a sole foreign supplier. But while a joint venture would immediately enhance our cash flow and strengthen our balance sheet—a simple and elegant solution—it was not only risky but fraught with danger should it fail. If our negotiations were publicized, national policies might harden and governments might well have intervened. Other companies might have entered the competition. And not the least concern was a revival of interest in breaking up ITT should the negotiations fail. We had much to win, but we also had much to lose.

We had been having conversations with one firm—the Nixdorf Computer Company. Heinz Nixdorf and I had a meeting at the company headquarters in Paderborn, West Germany, in early December 1985, but I felt it was unlikely we would be able to form an effective combination. A joint venture would not provide a European majority-owned entity in telecommunications. In view of our ownership of Standard Electrik Lorenz (SEL) in West Germany, ITT could not grant a majority to Nixdorf, so the combination would have been challenged by Germany's cartel laws. Our talks with Burroughs, Sperry, and Wang had not reached fruition, and an alliance with Nixdorf would pose different but equally difficult obstacles.

Georges Pebereau of Compagnie Générale d'Electricité and I were each modeling a telecommunications joint venture, and the ITT board approved the strategy of an ITT minority position. My position with the board was that the joint venture should be somewhere between 51 and 70 percent CGE-owned, and that CGE had to pay cash for the ITT shares. We valued ITT's telecommunications business to become part of the joint venture at $3.3 to $3.9 billion, with a book value of $1.6 billion. CGE would have control and the purchase would take place while the French Government owned CGE.

I stressed throughout our talks that any leak about the nature of our discussions would destroy the deal, particularly our willingness to be a minority partner. So a code name for our secret activity with CGE—"Roxane"—came from either the Morgan Stanley or the Lazard Frères office in Paris. The name was known initially to about ten people, a number that would grow ultimately to about fifty people. Before Roxane was unveiled to the public, ITT and CGE would be at the altar, with vows recorded in the world press.

After an extensive discussion of Roxane during the November 1985 ITT meetings—Capital Committee, Executive Committee, and full board—I was authorized to proceed.

I had talked with Ken Olson of Digital Equipment Corporation (DEC) on three different occasions about joint ventures, but none of these discussions promised a role that was beneficial for ITT with an infusion of cash to improve the balance sheet significantly. A relationship with the Swedish firm L. M. Ericsson, or AT&T, or Siemens seemed to be patently impossible because of market conditions, cartel regulations in West Germany, and the position of AT&T in the United States. In addition, AT&T had already teamed up with Philips in Europe. CGE, camouflaged as Roxane, was the one I wanted. The joint venture would give us back the French market that had been nationalized and would place the new company in the strongest market position in the world. In the competitive field of telecommunications, it would have dynamic leadership in switching, telephone subsets, cables, and perhaps even transmission.

It was an exciting possibility: Georges Pebereau and I had been gingerly leading up to the valuation of ITT's telecommunication holdings since a dinner meeting in Paris in July of 1985. We had completed exhaustive studies of our telecommunications networks worldwide and of the assets we had employed. I had concluded that a minimum valuation, a worst-case valuation, would be $2 billion for the entire activity; an acceptable valuation, $3.3 billion; an optimal valuation, $4 billion. In 1984, all of ITT's companies together, including telecommunications, had a market value of almost $4 billion, equivalent to an optimal valuation for only telecommunications in 1985. It would be possible to nearly double the value of the corporation with a highly successful sale.

Next, I went to Mexico in late 1985 in an attempt to calm Teléfonos de México (Telmex), our customer there. Telmex had been very understanding of the problems we were having with our System 12 switching. Most of the problems dealt with customizing the Mexican network to full digitalization in order to permit the highest degree of voice/data integration. There were problems we had not encountered in the European networks, but they were significant to the country that was still recovering from the major earthquake of the preceding spring.

I visited exchanges around the Mexico City area and then met with Emilio Carrillo, the head of Teléfonos de México, who was also a board member of our Mexican company, INDETEL, and a longtime friend of ITT. Carrillo was under great pressure because of our slow performance in installing System 12, but he assured me of continued support. Thus, in my meeting with Georges Pebereau at CGE headquarters in Paris in mid-November, I was able to advise him that the situation in Mexico for System 12 was being rectified.

That meeting turned out to be crucial. I proposed developing a joint venture in which CGE might have a majority participation. Georges sat up straight, wide-eyed behind his small rimmed glasses. Roxane was as attractive to him as to me. He saw that in one single act France would be thrust into the premier position in telecommunications. He could not sit still or contain his excitement.

I said, "You are going to have to consider a valuation of something like $3.9 to $4 billion for ITT's telecommunications business, so if ITT keeps 30 percent of Roxane, CGE will have to pay about $2.7 billion for 70 percent. The $2.7 billion would include the assumption of about $800 million of debt."

Georges stared at me probingly. Then he looked to the side, shrugged his shoulders, and stood up quickly to shake hands. "We have a lot to do before we seriously talk price. We are now partners."

Immediately he arranged meetings for me with Etienne Davignon, former president of the European Economic Community (EEC) and now a managing director of Société Générale, one of the largest banks in Belgium and France. Georges also wanted to organize meetings with Raymond Barre and Jacques Chirac, outside the current government, and with Edith Cresson and other people in the Mitterrand administration at the Elysée Palace.

Georges was particularly impressed by the fact that the ITT board—including Michel David-Weill, a most respected French banker—had given the approval for going forward on the basis of French majority ownership, and, most important, the majority ownership being held by the French Government itself.

He said, "I cannot tell any details to my Board of Directors, which represents the French government. But I assure you that the right people, of both parties, will know of our general approach. It is best for the moment not to tell them that CGE will own a majority. That might create premature waves."

Meanwhile, Georges, caught up in the romance of Roxane, had neglected to tell me that the award of 16 percent of the French market to AT&T had again been delayed. I left Paris for Zurich, feeling we had triggered what could become one of the great strategic moves in the history of ITT. Roxane could be the most significant transaction for ITT since Sosthenes Behn purchased all of AT&T's overseas telephone companies and equipment manufacturers in 1925.

In Zurich, we celebrated the fiftieth anniversary of ITT's Standard Telephone and Radio (STR) with leading members of the government and of the Swiss PTT. The PTT had selected System 12 as one of three systems for Switzerland. At the mansion of the president of Switzerland, STR's managing director, Werner Thierstein, and I joined the president in cutting a three-yard-long Swiss chocolate cake—which went well with champagne.

I liked Werner Thierstein. He knew the value of every Swiss franc he controlled. He loved the Swiss expression, "My favorite color is yellow, but I prefer yellow gold to yellow cheese; gold does not smell." Trim, formal, and a competent yodeler, Werner spoke English as well as French and German. I knew he would support Roxane, but he would have to wait seven months to learn of her.

My next stop was Brussels, to approve European company budgets for 1986. At a luncheon with Etienne Davignon and Gene Van Dyck, managing director of BTM, our company in Belgium, we discussed market shares in Belgium. Gene was generally aware of joint-venture talks with CGE and knew that Davignon was a CGE consultant, but I told neither one of the plan that CGE might take the majority. Everyone assumed ITT would retain a majority—a fact that was the biggest guardian of Roxane's secret. Belgium was important to Roxane, as was the Federal Republic of Germany.

Dr. Karlheinz Kaske, the head of Siemens, Germany's largest industrial company, had invited Helmut Lohr, managing director of Standard Electrik Lorenz, and me to have lunch with him at Siemens's Munich headquarters. Siemens was jealous of SEL's success and wanted nothing better than a takeover of ITT that would pull the financial rug out from under SEL. We had a friendly, somewhat sparring lunch conversation, during which Dr. Kaske fished for information without much success.

Upon my return to New York, Felix Rohatyn, Michel David-Weill, Howard Aibel, Cab Woodward, Bob Smith, and I reviewed my discussions in Europe. All but Bob Smith were excited about the prospects with CGE. Bob thought we would never get a fair price. John Chluski, an ITT senior vice president and my personal representative on the boards of several ITT majority-owned companies in Europe, had done the market-share studies, which clearly indicated the joint venture would capture about 42 to 43 percent of the European telecommunications market and would have $12 billion of revenues, with a heavy orientation in office products in Europe and in the United States. The joint venture would be the principal worldwide telecommunications competitor with complementary markets of CGE in French West Africa, ITT in East Africa and North Africa. We had complementing strong positions in the Middle East; good distribution of products in India, China, and

Australia, and other nations in the Far East. It was an excellent fit, and we all knew it.

During this same time period, Ed Carpenter commissioned a study by Booz Allen Hamilton to determine whether or not we should continue with our System 12 switching investment in the United States. The system was costing too much to develop for a United States market that was shrinking for its applications. I felt that Georges Pebereau would have no problem with a sound decision either way.

One other avenue still remained open. It was related directly to technical and market expansion of System 12. Nixdorf was the only computer company that was effectively integrating digital data and digital communications, and I did not want to leave the Nixdorf connection unexplored. John Chluski and I went to Paderborn to meet with Heinz Nixdorf—a walking legend to all, including his engaging deputy and heir apparent, Klaus Luft. Nixdorf walked us through his plants, greeting his workers. He discussed his company openly, and I reciprocated. It was apparent that he hoped to organize some kind of combination with ITT on a worldwide basis. On the other hand, it was equally clear that Nixdorf was not going to be involved in a business venture in Germany that he did not control. As a result, I was somewhat pessimistic about reaching an acceptable conclusion. We shook hands, agreeing only to pursue discussions in a more specific way in 1986, and John Chluski and I were once again off to Paris.

I went from Le Bourget Airport directly to a meeting with Jacques Chirac, mayor of Paris. His RPR (Rally Party of the Republic) was readying for the March 1986 elections. Seated in a high-backed, heavily stuffed chair in the mayor's palace, Chirac was tall and thin. He smoked his cigarettes in a relaxed, diffident fashion. Chirac was easy to talk to and had been well prepared by Georges Pebereau. It was a pleasure to see that 1981's negative attitude about ITT had completely dissipated, and there seemed to be a genuine wish to have us back.

John Chluski and I had a follow-up meeting with Georges Pebereau and François de Laage, his assistant, at our New York headquarters. We talked some about valuations, but mainly we discussed schedules and matters that would have to be attended to in early 1986. We agreed that while we could continue discussions, no final decision could be made until after the French elections in March— and, from my point of view, until after the ITT annual meeting in May.

Our goal was to continue to pursue an effective joint venture without getting to the point where public disclosure was required. Then, after the elections in France, which were expected to go to Chirac's party, we could determine a schedule of meetings, including consideration of the ITT annual meeting. Both sides knew it was essential to reach a decision by June 30, 1986. Roxane was too spectacular to remain hidden. Georges also wanted a June 30 deadline in view of decisions related to bringing AT&T into France for the 16 percent market share, and an AT&T transmission relationship with CIT Alcatel, a subsidiary of CGE.

AT&T must have been nonplussed and confused by the constant delays. The AT&T decision was now scheduled for June 30, 1986, delayed from June 30, 1985. We had something to do with that delay. Events now were on a collision course for June 30, but the Roxane decision dwarfed the AT&T one. Georges and I agreed to proceed carefully and confidentially with our next meetings, scheduled for early in 1986. We each kept a list of names of people who knew Roxane.

John Chluski and I realized that we were in for a long series of meetings that, if successful, would lead to continuous negotiations in Paris for at least a month; my 1986 schedule was already a shambles.

In mid-December 1985, Jessie and I attended an American Museum of Natural History event entitled "Diamonds and Spurs," highlighting the Anschutz art collection. At a table near ours were the Pritzkers, the Anschutzes, and the Geneens. Harold had told me a couple of months earlier that Pritzker had complained about me in Chicago when he still held ITT's stock. Geneen told Pritzker, "You have nothing to complain about, you have a good gain." And that was that for Harold—no minced words, no attempt to be ingratiating.

Jessie and I had invited one of the ITT directors, Ralph Davidson, and his wife, Lou, to the museum event. Ralph, who had never made any mention in several board meetings about knowing Phil Anschutz, inquired, "Say, Rand, would you like to meet Phil?" Jessie and I went over with him and Lou and met Phil and his wife, Nancy. Anschutz said, "You know, Rand, this lady is your biggest fan." I smiled and said, "Nancy, you must be the smartest member of the family." We all laughed. I thought later that perhaps Nancy helped keep Phil's activities in perspective.

Jay and Cindy Pritzker did not get up, nor did I go over to them. I just gave the Geneens a wave and went back to our table with Ralph, who said, "I'm sorry you had not met him before. I felt Phil Anschutz was not the type to be doing the kind of things you were concerned about. I think when he found out what really was going on, he got out of it quickly."

At ITT's office Christmas party on December 20, we toasted the holidays and the new year. Howard Aibel, Cab Woodward, Juan Cappello, and I toasted, most enthusiastically, Kathy, Helen, Jean, Jessie, and Roxane.

18

Defense Secrets

We were approaching a critical decision on our North American telecommunications efforts with System 12. The Booz Allen management consultants were evaluating the situation. I told the board that there would be a lot of flak, hand-wringing, and chortling if we did close down, but those elements would not hinder our making the right decision. I also briefed the board on developments related to CGE, and particularly about the schedule of decision-making and negotiations up to June 30, 1986.

On January 12, 1986, Booz Allen made its first presentation, which clearly indicated that they would be recommending suspension of System 12 switching activity in the United States. It appeared that ITT would only obtain an unprofitable third place at best in the saturated American market, after AT&T and Northern Telecommunications. Later in January I met with Michel David-Weill and Felix Rohatyn to discuss CGE. We agreed that the CGE joint venture was the right one, but that Northern Telecommunications could be brought into the act. Northern Telecom, previously discounted as a joint-venture partner, had been suggested by Booz Allen as a possible vehicle for staying in the North American telecommunications market. They would be an alternate bidder and keep the proper pressure on CGE. I knew that both Felix and Michel, especially Michel, had their hearts set on the CGE deal: I admired their agreeing to have a competitive bidder in the wings. Certainly they knew that under such circumstances, anything could happen.

Next, I went on to Norway for a series of meetings with Prime Minister Kare Willoch and the chairman of the Norwegian Telecommunications Administration, Mr. Kjell Holler, concerning System 12. The earlier Norwegian decision to go with System 12, to be built by ITT Standard Telefon OG Kabelfabrik (STK), for their entire telephone network weighed heavily on them, and they wanted to be sure I felt that weight also—which I did.

En route from Oslo to Brussels for a European Telecom Advisory Council meeting, I received word to go immediately to the ITT Tower on Avenue Louise. When I arrived at the office, I was told that Ed Carpenter wished to see me immediately, so I met with him and several ITT attorneys. Apparently, Standard Electrik Lorenz was about to be notified by the German Ministry of Defense that SEL could no longer receive classified information from the United States Department of Defense. These written orders were to come from Secretary Caspar Weinberger to U.S. Ambassador Richard Burt in Bonn for transmittal to the German minister of defense.

The potential damage was monumental. There would be no way to keep that action private while we tried to find a solution. Information provided to the United States Department of Defense through a Soviet defector indicated, on the surface, that a serious security leak existed at SEL. Our own investigation had shown no evidence that SEL was at fault, but ITT had been allowed no time with Assistant Secretary Richard Perle or Secretary Weinberger to prove it. They had made no effort to let us know about an investigation that had been going on since September of 1985. Furthermore, our own Standard Electrik people, including Helmut Lohr, thought they had answered all of the questions successfully, and therefore they had not red-flagged the security matter to ITT head-quarters in Brussels.

We did not know the details of the Soviet defector's statements, but those statements had to be extremely damaging. We felt the defector's testimony was erroneous, either unintentionally or purposefully, but we were in no position to counter it. More than anyone else in the room, I understood the far-reaching, uncontrollable, and even terrible consequences of disclosure of this Weinberger decision to the world press. ITT again would be on the front pages of every newspaper in the Western world.

Our stock was still in the mid-30s, and just as we had gotten the raiders out of our stock, this incident could put our company back into play. Certainly, ITT's overall security clearance would be placed in jeopardy, if not canceled. There would be extreme financial consequences in addition to the public damage to the company. I listened to the details carefully, went through everything with our people as they presented it, and concluded that we were being treated unfairly. We had to convince Secretary Weinberger to hold up his action until we could defend our position.

A meeting of the Ministry of Defense with German industrial contractors had already occurred, without SEL. We had to move quickly or competitors would have our exclusion on the front pages before we had a chance to state our case. I called Secretary Weinberger's office right away and told his secretary it was urgent that I talk with him, that I was in Brussels but I would stay right at the telephone until he returned my call.

One half hour later, Secretary Weinberger called back. I summarized: "Cap, I've been through this entire security situation relating to SEL. I am extremely concerned, as this could be devastating to ITT if your decision were to go forward. I must have an opportunity to talk to you to explain our point of view and to offer every cooperation. This is the first I have heard of it. You know if you had called me down I would have given every cooperation, but your investigation has been going on completely independent of us. I understand you have information that is not available to us, but I believe even that information is in many respects just intended to create problems between Germany and the United States. I really believe that ITT and SEL are innocent in this matter, and I will fly immediately back to meet with you."

He had listened. Then he said, "Rand, we are concerned about the way German contractors have been handling our classified information. We think some lessons need to be taught." I replied, "Yes, but this would be extremely unfair to dump this on ITT and ITT only until you have really heard us out."

Weinberger said, "I understand, Rand, but the order is going to stay." I asked, "When will it finally be released?"

He said, "It is in process now. I would say that by the end of next week, it should be in Germany." I replied, "Secretary Weinberger, I implore you to hold up that decision, to hold that action with the U.S. ambassador in Bonn until I can see you."

He said, "We will hold it until I see you, but that does not mean it will not go forward." "I understand that, sir," I responded. "I'll be in your office whenever you say."

He concluded, "Twelve o'clock on Monday."

"I'll be there."

We received further briefings from our German contingent. Ed Carpenter and I were confident the information the SEL people had presented was true: A disclosure apparently had occurred concerning classified data, but it did not seem to be an SEL violation. Rather, it seemed to be a problem in another country that could be handled only by our Department of Defense authorities in the country involved.

That night, deeply troubled, I flew to Rome for a dinner with Professor Romano Prodi, the head of the Istituto per la Riconstruzione Industriale (IRI), the huge government-owned conglomerate that ran everything from steel-making to shipbuilding. IRI owned STET, the electronics conglomerate, which in turn owned the Italian telephone operating company (SIP), and the telephone equipment company (Italtel). The firm had sales of more than $30 billion a year, and, for the first time, was nearing break-even because of Professor Prodi's successes. He was an extremely relaxed, interesting man whose title fitted him perfectly. Short and heavy, with black tousled hair, he slouched easily and confidently in his easy chair. His facial expressions were unique, from heavy eyebrow-raising to lips that said, "so . . ." in a way that implied he knew your ancestry as well as your subject matter.

Prodi believed in international alliances, but he was pressing me on FACE's role in telecommunications versus the role of the IRI-owned Italtel, headed by a shrewd Italian woman, Marisa Bellisario. He restated the basic Italian theory that they wanted only two telephone switching systems: one an Italtel system and one either an L. M. Ericsson, ITT, or GTE system. They simply had not decided, but one or two might have to be pulled out of the competition. It was a gentle threat. I got his attention by offering to sell him shares in FACE. When we parted company, he looked more quizzical than assured. The next day, I had meetings with Dr. Michele Principe, the vice chairman of STET, and with Paolo Benzoni, the head of SIP. Both were constructive meetings in which FACE was praised as a supplier to SIP. I left for Paris feeling reasonably relaxed about Italy, but not about Secretary Weinberger.

I arrived in Paris in time to have a two-hour meeting with Georges Pebereau, during which John Chluski and I confirmed our discussions with the ITT board. I indicated that we were seriously considering, on a confidential basis, discontinuing our System 12 operations in the United States. I told him I wanted to be sure that such a decision would not be disruptive to our joint-venture discussions. He assured me that the decision would not bother him at all. In fact, he said, "I would regard it as a favorable development. The United States market is too tough."

At 9 A.M. on Monday, January 27, 1986, Helmut Lohr, Howard Aibel, and a few others gathered in ITT's Washington office. We huddled all morning to prepare our case for Secretary Weinberger.

When we arrived at his office on the Pentagon's third floor just before noon, I was told I would have to be brief, that the Secretary had inserted this meeting into a busy schedule and had only a few minutes to spend with me.

After I greeted him, he responded, "Hello, Rand. I'm sorry about these circumstances, but you understand we're going to have to make an example of somebody to make sure that our classified information is protected by those German contractors."

Several people were with him—Undersecretary of the Army James R. Ambrose; Assistant Secretary Richard Perle; his legal counsel; his military aide. Howard Aibel was with me; Helmut Lohr and the others waited outside. We presented our story convincingly. As they listened, they seemed to realize the sincerity of ITT, the comprehensiveness of our rules and regulations, and our concern with protecting classified information. We insisted that the information received from the Soviet defector was erroneous and that we could refute it.

In spite of our presentation, there were staff comments that we should be disciplined and taught a lesson. Suddenly, the one person from whom I least expected support, Richard Perle, stepped into the conversation and said, "Mr. Secretary, why don't we stop the order until I can work on this with Mr. Araskog? There may be some things here we don't know, and I'd like to be sure we are careful. I do agree with Mr. Araskog that this could do severe damage to his corporation and even to our German relations. So I would like to go slow and I would like to investigate it thoroughly and get back to you."

Secretary Weinberger seemed surprised, and begrudgingly said, "Well, okay, Richard, I'll put that in your hands, but I want this resolved within two weeks, and if in two weeks I have no other answer, we are going to go ahead and implement the order. I want you to understand that."

Perle said he did. I think what he really understood was that Secretary Weinberger was saving face, and that was certainly all right with Howard and me.

Afterward, Howard and I met with Perle for several hours in an extremely productive discussion. He brought in his investigative team, which obviously had been totally convinced by the defector's information, despite the fact that it was genuinely in error.

It took us another month to put all of this behind us, to convince everyone that ITT and Standard Electrik Lorenz had in no way participated in the leak of information. A leak had in fact occurred, but it had not been through the SEL or ITT offices.

I wrote to Secretary Weinberger and Richard Perle after it was all over, thanking them for withholding their decision, thanking them for their cooperation and assuring them of ITT's continued support. There had been nothing since the July 2, 1984, Gerrity letter that had shaken me as much as the information about the Weinberger order. Interestingly enough, Richard Perle, who saved us from disaster, was most courteous, forgiving, and even apologetic later. I never heard more about the matter from Secretary Weinberger, but what could he say? I was glad it was over. After disposing of this challenge, Howard and I concluded that any raider who wanted to run ITT needed to have his head examined.

It may seem a small point in retrospect, but the raiders never fully appreciated just how delicate and complicated a corporation ITT is, with a great many government agencies monitoring its activities. Long-standing relationships facilitate the exchange of information with the regulatory bodies. If they are torn asunder by selling off component companies, business is likely to flounder and fail. And it is of the utmost importance for an international corporation to have the kind of presence that allows for access to the highest levels of government, and these contacts are not made in a fortnight. The raiders forgot that—or perhaps they never knew it.

At the February 1986 board meeting, we were able to report our success with the Defense Department. I had sought advice from Larry Eagleburger early on, and had alerted Dick Perkins so that he could alert other board members as appropriate. We had been concerned about the matter hitting the press and catching members by surprise, but even more concerned about a leak before the matter was disposed of to our satisfaction. It had caused a lot of anxious moments—an all-too-typical stormy January.

19

The Stalking Horse

If Roxane was to become more than an ephemeral dream—a vision lovely but lost—we would have to generate more pressure. Secrecy was all to our advantage, though an occasional leak or a rumor not denied was equally useful. Roxane meant love, but she also meant war. At West Point we had read von Clausewitz, who wrote that war was but a continuation of political relations. In February 1986, we added heat to our politics.

I had reckoned on System 12 to change the fortunes of the company dramatically. Some critics said it was a bet-the-company decision, that it was reckless and a nonstarter. They were wrong; it was an outstanding achievement. System 12 initially was my baby. In the late 1970s, the Swedish company L. M. Ericsson had had a breakthrough in telecommunications with digital switching, a successful development that threatened to grab a significant share of ITT's European markets. We had to leapfrog their technology: Developing a better digital switchboard became a $1 billion priority. We created a team whose technical expertise was second to none, and our scientists created System 12—a digital switchboard with virtually unlimited capacity in voice, data, and distributed control from terminals that reduce or bypass central processing units. The modular design was easy to adopt in many foreign networks. We won virtually all the technical shoot-outs we entered, and System 12 was accepted worldwide—except in the United States.

We missed the boat in the United States because we first had to protect our market share in Europe. We did not anticipate the sudden breakup of AT&T and the early opening it offered us. While we concentrated on Europe, Northern Telecommunications had moved into the U.S. market with its advanced switchboards. In addition, we also faced GTE, Stromberg-Carlson, NEC, and Siemens. Regardless of our acknowledged triumphs abroad, the Baby Bell systems were hard nuts to crack, since their electronic logic and networks were basically different from our European technology. It took time and money to adapt, let alone run through the Bell System's extensive testing procedures. Setting up a marketing and sales force to be a major U.S. vendor was also costly. And decision time for Bell was short. In brief, the obstacles were formidable and the competition fierce.

By February 1986, it was clear that the U.S. market would not be profitable. We had definitely concluded that System 12 might never obtain a reasonable market share, considering all the other competition. Nevertheless, it remained a highly viable switchboard for the rest of the world. I again went to Mexico to reassure the Mexican Government of our performance. At that time, Emilio Carrillo, head of Telmex, had back on line almost all of the telephone connections he had lost in the serious earthquake of the preceding spring. It had been a tremendous blow to the telecommunications network in Mexico, but it was a credit to Teléfonos de México that they had put everything back in order.

From Mexico City, I went to Nashville, Tennessee, where I had arranged a 4 P.M. Sunday meeting at the home of Ed Fitzgerald, the head of Northern Telecommunications. A big man with an engaging and disarming laugh, Ed had just celebrated his sixtieth birthday. He was joined by Derek Davies, his senior vice president for corporate development, a slight man who knew the telecommunications business inside and out. After I indicated to them ITT's serious interest in selling a majority or a minority of its telecommunications operations worldwide, we discussed the opportunities and problems that would accompany such a transaction.

Northern Telecom, a Canadian-based spinoff of Bell Canada, was a rapidly growing power in the United States. Ed felt his company was doing reasonably well penetrating Europe; it had entered Japan with more horsepower than any other U.S. supplier. Overall, it was clear to both of us that we had complementary capabilities if they could be put together. They had North America and Japan and we had Europe, Africa, Latin America, and China.

There were, of course, some inherent snags. We had incompatible digital systems, both of which were very advanced. There were potential problems with management. These were matters we both wanted to think about, but the gem had been dropped in Ed Fitzgerald's hands, and he was planning to examine it carefully. I emphasized that the Northern Telecom–ITT talks had to be conducted in complete secrecy. They were aware that we were talking to CGE. Ed replied, "You bet. For our sake, too." Then he added, "Look, Rand, those Frenchmen don't pay—you know that."

We flew on to Boston, where ITT was having its February board meetings at Sheraton headquarters. In addition to the review of Sheraton, there were three major items on the agenda: First was a discussion of the status of the SEL/Weinberger affair and our belief that it would be resolved favorably. Second was a review of our System 12 situation. We now had two presentations by Booz Allen confirming their opinion, shared by our own management, that we should stop our System 12 activity in North America. Their reasoning was that even if we succeeded with the development program, System 12 installation would be so late that Northern Telecom's and AT&T's digital equipment would be firmly implanted. There would be little market left for ITT, and we would never recover our investment. It was pointless to proceed. Even the general manager of the System 12 activity in Raleigh, North Carolina, could not argue with the results of the study. So we told the board about our decision and indicated that we would make the termination announcement on Thursday, February 13.

The third major item concerned my meeting with Ed Fitzgerald in Nashville, Tennessee, and the fact that we now had introduced Northern Telecom as another potential partner in telecommunications. I reported that I had taken this step after discussions with Michel David-Weill and Felix Rohatyn. The board was quite pleased to have another potential suitor to ensure that we obtained the best deal for ITT. I also advised the directors about my meeting with Etienne Davignon, emphasizing that we could count on full support from Belgium for a CGE joint venture. BTM's 85 percent market share in Belgium would be supported by Davignon and the people he represented at Société Générale.

The announcement that we were stopping our System 12 activity in North America brought instant accolades from the analysts, the rating agencies, and the stock market. Cries of "What will ITT do now?" came from the business press. At the same time, we reported the results for the year. We took a $105 million write-off for our American telecommunications effort. I wished it had been otherwise, of course, but I think it was worth the effort. And it was more imperative than ever to bolster our financial condition. For fiscal year 1985, our net income was down 34 percent, from $448 million to $294 million, although revenues were up 11 percent over 1984. Selling off a major portion of our worldwide telecommunications would bring in substantial profits for our balance sheet if the price was right. It was important that we press on toward a solution.

Interest in ITT was rekindled by some European companies such as Bosch and Siemens. Professor Hans L. Merkle and Dr. Marcus Bierich of Bosch came to call on me, as did Dr. Kaske of Siemens. All were curious about what ITT would do next, and all remained curious after our meetings.

In March, rumors were beginning to hum around Europe, and particularly in Italy, about various international telecommunications alliances being contemplated. Siemens and GTE were supposedly joining forces, ITT was believed to be considering sales of some of its majority interests in companies in Europe. A variety of stories linked companies with ITT, but no one focused on CGE and ITT.

The underground whispered that the wistful, mercurial, unscheduled, energetic Frenchman Georges Pebereau could not possibly be thinking of an alliance with his most hated competitor, the disciplined ITT. No, Pebereau was aligning with Italtel, Plessey, and perhaps Siemens, to destroy ITT's market share in Europe. There were some rumors about ITT discussions with Northern Telecom, but they were still below the noise level. ITT and CGE were running without lights. No one knew what was happening. Now Northern Telecom was out there too, also running in darkness. It was working, and there were only three months to go. We just had to keep the ships in line, know where each was and where we were. Not easy.

After the March 16 elections in France, we reviewed the results. The new government was very positive toward Georges Pebereau and CGE. (In early 1987, CGE would be one of the first companies to be privatized.) The new government was generally aware of Pebereau's discussions with me, since we had also met with Jacques Chirac and others. As a result, they were familiar with a joint-venture plan. But Georges did not think it appropriate for me to have meetings with the new government officials. He thought that should come later, after he had executed a definitive agreement. His judgment had been implicitly correct thus far, so his advice was acceptable. That judgment might one day cost Georges Pebereau his job, but surely it saved Roxane from an early death. No one but Georges knew the price that I insisted on extracting for ITT's telecommunications activity.

At our New York office, we held one of our best meetings ever with Standard & Poor's, during which they reconfirmed our credit ratings. They believed firmly that the decision to stop the System 12 effort in North America would strengthen the balance sheet of the company.

The next week, during our board meetings, we updated the directors on the situation in France, indicating that in the near future we also would be holding a crucial meeting with Northern Telecommunications. Their people had been studying our data carefully and were showing considerable interest in buying a large part of the telecommunications activities, about 70 percent. They wanted full management control, but they had not thought through how they would hold their potential acquisition together. Europe wanted European control rather than control out of North America, and this was still a high hurdle for Northern Telecom. But their computers were whirling, working out ways to do it, and Derek Davies was indeed a clever man.

A limited number of ITT management personnel—probably only about ten or so—had been involved in our considerations of Northern Telecom and CGE. The information had been tightly controlled by Lazard, and we had not retained outside counsel. Georges Pebereau was exercising the same tight control. Suddenly I was advised by our people that CGE was disseminating an anti–System 12 white paper to our worldwide customers. The white paper decried System 12 as being a system on paper only, as opposed to the well-tried and effective E-10 switching systems produced by CGE's subsidiary company, CIT Alcatel. That hurt.

Outraged, I called Georges Pebereau to complain. Georges asked, understandably, "Rand, what do you want me to do? I've told no one about what we are discussing except the limited group of people of whom you are aware. Our people down the line are continuing to do what they think they should do competitively to beat System 12." Whether or not I liked their white-paper tactics, I had to concede that CGE's stand was super camouflage for Roxane, who otherwise would have been a cover story for the media in all the capitals of Europe.

While CGE was "trashing" our best product, some American investment bankers were helping raiders trash American corporations. ITT had had an identity problem from its early years: Americans thought it was European; Europeans were certain it was an American corporation operating abroad, but were confused because it was full of Europeans. There was some truth in both perceptions. Sosthenes Behn had the foresight to maintain production plants abroad to supply the telephone systems. These naturally were manned by local labor, technicians, and engineers. At the same time, his managers and executives were occasionally transplanted Americans mixed in with prominent nationals. He was aware that it was good politics and smart diplomacy to be truly international, so he relied on establishment talent in foreign countries. Hence, the confusion of identity, but Behn's foresight saved ITT from many radical backlashes and calls for nationalization of foreign interests. Nevertheless, the ambiguity remained—our own government often treated us as if we were foreign, and so did the Europeans, for all the "local" content.

We had no sooner beaten off the pirates at home when we found a senior executive of an American brokerage house beckoning Europeans to join in the hostile takeover game. I had been invited to participate at a CEO International Roundtable at Villa d'Este on Lake Como, Italy, sponsored by Arthur Andersen & Co., Bain & Co., Landor Associates, Metra Proudfoot International, and Merrill Lynch. I spoke on the first panel on the subject of "The CEO as the Global Strategist," and after my remarks, I dropped in to listen in on a discussion group entitled "A Strategic Approach to Mergers and Acquisitions." The panelists were Richard Grogan, a vice president of Bain & Co.; Kenneth Miller, then a managing director of Merrill Lynch Capital Markets, who now has left that firm; and Nahum Vaskevitch, the managing director of Merrill Lynch Capital Markets in London, who also has left the firm. Vaskevitch and Grogan had just completed their remarks, and Ken Miller came on. Then a senior partner of Merrill Lynch, Miller was trying to provoke European CEOs to join the takeover fun in the United States: "The Hansons are there. The Goldsmiths are there. Why not you?" He continued, "All American chief executive officers in the hands of raiders and investment bankers are like pigeons in the pigeon game. You know the pigeon game. The pigeon waits for a piece of candy to come down a chute, and after a while, after a piece of candy has come down every thirty seconds, he walks over to the slide whether the candy is coming down or not." It was an insufferably arrogant analogy.

Miller said that American CEOs were in constant fear of takeover, and that there was an uneven playing field that favored the raiders, both legally and in terms of SEC regulations. He stated that the Washington regulatory environment was such that anything was allowed; backs were turned on antitrust.

I waited until he had finished. "I'd like to address Mr. Miller, and this is not a question; it's a statement. I have sat here and listened to the stories you have told, Ken, and I find them untrue and self-serving." I went on. "It is not true that American chief executive officers spend all of their time worrying about takeover." Addressing the audience, I continued, "We are trying to build an economic environment that is positive. The playing field is leveling, and there is a tough attitude out there. I think it is unconscionable for a top executive of an American investment banking house to come over here and run down American corporations and try to tempt you into coming over to join what he calls a 'takeover battle' on a tilted playing field. I simply want all of you to understand that I'm here. I'm not sitting back there worrying about takeover. Our company has been about as famous or infamous as any with respect to raiders in our stock. Sure, I spent a lot of time defending the company when several raiders had large holdings in our stock at the same time, but that is not the norm for American corporations. We succeeded, and so can other companies who have the right spirit. Also, we paid no exorbitant legal or investment bankers' fees because we did not do anything rash like buying back shares or spinning off companies or making foolhardy mergers."

Miller was extremely defensive. He stuttered and attempted to respond by saying that Merrill Lynch was itself considered a take-over target, that he was not shooting at American business. But it was all pretty lame.

I returned to Paris for further meetings with Pebereau. We agreed we were far enough along to put everything on hold, except our own in-house studies, until after the ITT annual meeting, which would take place on Tuesday, May 13, 1986. After that, if everything was still on go, we would shift into high gear to complete negotiations by the end of June, or drop the whole matter.

Georges knew from Morgan Stanley that Northern Telecom was also a player, and he had advised the highest levels of the new government, in whom he had confidence, that he would be in tight competition. John Chluski had been questioned by Georges and had simply told the truth, that "several members of the ITT top management preferred Northern Telecom, but Rand Araskog was in charge and strongly favored CGE."

In Wolfsburg, West Germany, Dr. Hubertus von Gruenberg, of ITT Teves brake company, and Dr. Klaus Bleyer, of ITT SWF, joined me for meetings with Dr. Carl Hahn and Professor Ernst Fiala of Volkswagenwerk to support our Teves and SWF activities as major suppliers to Volkswagenwerk. ITT supplied more than $100 of product for each and every car manufactured in the Western world. Volkswagenwerk was one of our largest customers for brakes, antiskid systems, lights, windshield wipers, displays, switches, and small motors. So Dr. Hahn was important to us.

Hahn was in the process of divesting his data systems operation to Olivetti, and he clearly was intending to concentrate on his effective automobile operations. We walked the huge plant, walked a totally automatic car assembly line, and then lunched together. If the Roxane transaction was concluded successfully, ITT's automotive operations would be the largest product companies owned by ITT, and I could ill afford to neglect them now.

Back in New York at the end of April, we had a productive meeting with Northern Telecommunications. Ed Fitzgerald brought his chief financial officer, legal personnel, and the inimitable Derek Davies. Cab Woodward, Bob Smith, Ed Carpenter, and Howard Aibel joined me, and we met at my apartment for several hours. There were grave considerations related to disruption of ITT's telecommunications activities in Europe, if the acquisition of a majority of ITT by Northern Telecom was not done quickly and adroitly.

During the meeting, I had reached the conclusion that the only way ITT could sell to Northern Telecom was if Northern Telecom would hand us a certified check for the full purchase price for ITT telecommunications—a check we could cash immediately, leaving Northern Telecom to hold things together. But I did not tell them that. The European PTTs and governments, ITT's principal customers, could regard a sale of ITT's companies to another North American company as being antithetical to the principles of the EEC. Nevertheless, we wanted Northern Telecom to stay in the running, so I told Ed Fitzgerald we would have to hold everything in abeyance until after our annual meeting. He understood that, but Northern Telecom's fascination with ITT's telecommunications business lacked only a name like Roxane.

The sudden death of Heinz Nixdorf in Germany removed his corporation as a possibility for a joint venture. Without Nixdorf himself at the helm, and lacking his vision and feeling for what could be done with ITT, Klaus Luft, the new chairman, felt he first had to get his feet on the ground running the company. So we closed off that avenue and Nixdorf joined Wang, Burroughs, and Sperry as an experience in "nothing ventured, nothing gained."

We felt we were now on the right course, closing in on a major joint venture with another telecommunications company, European owned and European based. But we also still had a stalking horse, a powerful Canadian/American company, to assist us in expediting and finalizing the negotiations with CGE or picking up with us if the CGE deal somehow faltered.

20

Full Court Press

Our stalking horse was showing signs of restiveness. Rumors continued that ITT was in deep negotiations concerning its telecommunications sector. Ed Fitzgerald of Northern Telecommunications called my home early in June 1986 to check on the status of our talks. His first call was intercepted by my sixteen-year-old daughter Kathy's answering machine. Not wishing to miss any of her friends during school vacation, Kathy had plugged her system into the house lines. Fitzgerald was rather surprised to hear a soft, sultry voice breathing heavily and pleading, "Leave a message, leave a message, leave a message," with a background of rock music.

"I had to wonder, Rand, what kind of house you were running," Fitzgerald said, when he finally reached me. "We're wondering what is happening. We have heard rumors that you have gone quite far in Europe and just wanted to make sure we still had an opportunity as you said we would."

I replied, "Things have become quite serious there, and we are going to have to see them through to an end before I can talk to you further on the matter. We expect and hope to reach a final conclusion there, but we haven't done so as yet. I can't tell you anything more about it. However, if it does not work out, I'll certainly be back in touch with you.''

He indicated, understandably, that by then they might not be interested. ''Well, Ed,'' I said, ''if that's the way it is, so be it, but we're going to see this one through to a conclusion of some kind in Paris.''

I returned to Paris to intensify our efforts in continuous meetings at CGE headquarters with Georges Pebereau and his staff. Georges was a different man. He was edgy and his eyes darted around behind his small, round, silver-rimmed glasses. He would frequently run his hand through his thin hair, then lean far forward across the table and appeal to me. When it got to be too much for him, he would suddenly disappear and I would be given a variety of reasons for his actions. Once I was told that he was taking a subway somewhere—because he had never ridden on a subway and wanted to try it.

Back at our hotel, we would await his return. Hours later his staff reported: ''He became lost. After all, he had never been on a subway before.'' But then he would suddenly return, apparently refreshed.

The investment bankers were all active, and as of Saturday night, June 14, we were still far enough apart that I did not have information for the ITT board, which was scheduled to meet the following week in Oslo. After midnight, I laid down a final condition as to price for Georges Pebereau. If a resolution could be reached in line with that final stipulation, then I would take it to the ITT Board of Directors. Otherwise, Pebereau could expect that the deal would be off and negotiations would be over.

Pebereau accepted the condition, and I took a final price to Oslo. After considerable discussion and review, the board agreed to the terms and conditions that we had negotiated, and I returned to Paris to complete the deal. In essence, we achieved a total valuation of $3.9 billion of our telecommunications business worldwide—$26 per share of ITT common stock. It consisted of 30 percent of the joint venture, worth $1.3 billion; $1.8 billion in cash; and debt transfer of $800 million. These conditions certainly met our most optimistic expectations.

We had a good deal of legal terminology still to work out, along with some unresolved matters that could affect the price. Howard Aibel took complete charge. We worked on Wednesday, Thursday, and Friday, but by Thursday night we were in sufficiently good shape to have a champagne party and celebrate the results. At the gathering were Georges Pebereau, Pierre Suard (head of CGE's subsidiary, CIT Alcatel), Francois de Laage (Pebereau's assistant), Michel David-Weill, John Chluski, Howard Aibel, Charlie Goldman (an ITT associate general counsel), Remmert Laan of the Lazard Frères Paris office, and several others. We turned everything over to the attorneys for a weekend of work so we could meet again the following week for final initialing and my signature.

After a weekend in Italy, I learned that things had come apart again in Paris—champagne party or not. I returned to Paris, where we went back into negotiations. My feeling was that Morgan Stanley, representing CGE, had thrown a monkey wrench into the whole proceeding. Their managing partner, Bob Greenhill, wanted to talk with me. Howard Aibel was with me as Greenhill tried to explain what he had advised Pebereau.

Finally, I said, "You know, it seems I have to hit you with a hammer to get it through your head that our board approved all that it was willing to do. You want to continue to play around with this, go ahead and kill it, but know you did it. There is no more give, period. Now, why don't you talk with Michel and see if you can get this back on track, or I'm going home."

John Chluski called François de Laage to tell him the situation and to stipulate that, above all, the agreement had to be signed by June 30, 1986, or it would not be signed at all.

On June 24, working all day and into the evening, we ironed out the problems and had yet another champagne party. Thinking we had everything in place, I left the next morning for Brussels, where Dan Weadock was holding management reviews and all of our European management was gathered. I advised the managing directors that we were about to sign a major agreement with CGE, providing for a joint venture in which CGE would take the majority. There were looks of surprise and, in some cases, looks of dismay at the planned change in majority ownership. Rumors were rife all around Europe, but nothing was accurate. The managers had many questions: Helmut Lohr from Standard Electrik Lorenz, Gene Van Dyck from BTM, Miguel Canalejo from Spain, Umberto Ferroni from Italy. Finally, everyone began to acknowledge that this was right for ITT, agreeing that it could be the best thing for the ITT telecommunications companies in Europe. With the level of anxiety reduced, I returned to Paris for final meetings with Georges Pebereau. Ed Carpenter stayed behind to work out customer-notification plans with the managing directors. This would be big news in their home countries.

That night, I initialed and signed the agreement for ITT, and then Georges Pebereau initialed it. He could not sign it until the French Government, the principal owner of CGE, had approved the contract. We expected that it would be approved immediately. Georges Pebereau brought it to the attention of the Government on the evening of June 25.

After midnight that night, I was awakened at the Bristol Hotel. Michel David-Weill was calling, in deep distress—he said the French Government would not approve the agreement as written. I joined him in dismay and dejection.

Michel indicated that evidently Pebereau had not done enough to pave the way with the minister of industry, Alain Madelin, or with the minister of finance and economy, Edouard Baladur—and, therefore, with new Prime Minister Jacques Chirac. The size of the transaction caught them totally by surprise; they had an inadequate understanding of the magnitude of the endeavor and the implications for other European countries.

The next morning, Georges and I reconvened. He was extremely upset and walked in circles, talking to himself. The date of June 30 was on the document as a drop-dead date—both as I had initialed and signed it and as he had initialed it. He was embarrassed, but he told me that Roxane still could be saved, that the Minister of Industry wanted to see me right away. So on Thursday, June 26, Minister of Industry Alain Madelin met with John Chluski, Charles Goldman of Howard Aibel's staff, and me at eleven in the morning. Madelin was young and confident; his staff members took notes throughout the meeting. He spoke alternately casually and intently, slightly condescendingly, but not enough to be offensive. Madelin wanted to discuss the contract we had signed, so we went through a long explanation of the history of the negotiations, the strengths we saw in the agreement, and the benefits for CGE, for ITT, and for France.

When we were finished, Minister Madelin said they understood all this; they knew a great deal of work had gone into it, but they wanted to modify the agreement. I told him that the agreement had to stand as signed, that it had been in the works for months— indeed, that we had begun talking fifteen months earlier. I explained that negotiations had been difficult and that each side had compromised to its limit. I said that, as far as I was concerned, if any comma were removed, if any *t* were uncrossed, if any *i* were undotted, the agreement would be null and void. They could make no change now.

Minister Madelin seemed frustrated. Charles Goldman and John Chluski had been with me at almost all of the meetings with Georges Pebereau, and now each confirmed what I had said in French and in more detail. As a result of this absolutely firm position on our part, Minister Madelin said, "I have to think about it further. I have to talk to Minister Baladur, and he would have to have some time to consider it."

We regarded the outcome as positive. Obviously they saw the French magic in the deal and did not want to lose it: They were beginning to get used to Roxane's attractiveness, if not her price.

Details of the agreement hit the press in France, and then a front-page article appeared in the *New York Times*. The coverage was very complimentary to the deal and highlighted the telecommunications power that France would become through this transaction. Pressure was on the French Government not to ruin the deal.

Indeed, on reflection, the price became the sticking point. The French Government would be obliged to come up with 5 billion French francs if the deal were to go forward. That was no small sum for a new government to have thrust on it without a chance to negotiate. It was as much a matter of money as it was a matter of national prestige.

That afternoon, around five in the evening, I was asked to see Minister Baladur at the Finance Ministry, together with Michel David-Weill. Baladur had worked for one of CGE's companies and was now next in line to Prime Minister Chirac. His huge, ancient office had a dusty atmosphere, made beautiful by the sunlight beaming through the French doors to the garden. He moved and talked slowly, regally. For someone recently in office, the rococo chair suited him. Shifting from French to English and back easily and without losing the ambience of the conversation, Baladur again raised the issue of reopening the negotiations and I repeated everything I had said before—in a polite but absolutely firm manner. He told me they had to have time to consider the agreement, and he did not feel the June 30 deadline allowed sufficient time. He requested an extension to the end of July.

I said no, that ITT stock had climbed $1.2 billion since the details of the transaction had been leaked to the press. I reminded them that we had kept this whole matter confidential until the day we submitted the agreement to the French Government, and one day later, it was leaked to the French press and now was in the American press. Baladur's response to that was a shrug of his shoulders, saying, "Well, what did you expect?"

Michel David-Weill was extremely helpful in the discussions, making it clear that we could not countenance any change in the contract. When I agreed to extend the termination date only to July 4, Minister Baladur accepted. But he wanted us to talk to Georges Pebereau, and he hoped we would reconsider the extension to July 31. I said that July 4 was the limit. Then Michel and I shook hands with Baladur and departed. As we left, we noticed that Georges Pebereau's car was parked outside the building. Of course, we had suspected that Pebereau would be meeting with Baladur after we left. Baladur had good reasons, which he had not disclosed to us, for needing the extension: One involved the future of Georges Pebereau; the other concerned the financing for the huge transaction.

When I returned to the United States, I called Howard Aibel. On the plane, I had realized that in view of the way ITT's stock had risen with the news of the CGE joint venture, there was no way I could insist on a final decision by July 4. The probability was that if I did insist, the French Government would not approve the deal. Balancing the facts, I concluded that I would have to grant the French a reasonable amount of time to consider the transaction, and that would be until July 31. Through Michel David-Weill, we communicated this to the French Government on Tuesday, July 1. The French then began excruciating reviews of all of the specifics of the transaction—the financial portion, the market shares, and the reaction of other countries to Roxane.

On Thursday, July 3, I attended a Council on Foreign Relations meeting in New York, at which French President François Mitterrand was the principal speaker. The socialist government clearly supported the deal. On the Fourth of July at 7:30 A.M., Jessie and I boarded Malcolm Forbes's *Highlander* with a large group of people to spend the next fifteen hours or so watching the tall ships and the other events of the celebration featuring the refurbished Statue of Liberty. At one point during the day, the *Highlander* pulled back to the pier so Madame Mitterrand could board the vessel and greet everyone. When she came by the spot where I was standing, Malcolm introduced me, beaming that I was waiting with great anticipation for the conclusion of the fantastic telecommunications deal with CGE in her country. Mrs. Mitterrand, if she understood, showed no great emotion about it one way or the other, but Malcolm played up the meeting anyway in the next issue of *Forbes*.

The following weekend, we were off to Cap d'Antibes for a summer vacation, but it turned out to be more work than vacation. After only two days, I flew to Madrid for meetings with Luis Solana, president of Compañía Telefónica Nacional de España (CTNE), to be sure he understood my position on the joint venture and to do my part in bringing Spain into it. Compañía Telefónica, the telephone operating company of Spain, owned 20 percent of ITT's Standard Electrica; it was extremely important that our relations be good in a country where we had a huge market share. We were also particularly hopeful, or at least I was, that CTNE would decide to invest $300 million in the joint venture—a 7 percent interest. This investment would match one by Société Générale in Belgium. I felt that Belgium and Spain—where we had market shares of 85 percent and 75 percent, respectively—were countries where Roxane would be well served by major domestic investments.

Luis Solana was unusually high-spirited. A handsome, youthful man with wavy black hair, well dressed and in excellent condition, Luis prided himself on his press relations and his ability to make deals. Miguel Canalejo and Manuel Marquez Balin, our two top Spanish executives, attended the meeting with me. Solana was complimentary about the ITT/CGE deal. He said it had taken only six hours for him to obtain approval from Prime Minister Felipe Gonzalez to invest the $300 million.

I had authorized Georges Pebereau to talk to two people about investing in the joint venture prior to our signing and initialing the agreement in late June: Etienne Davignon of Société Générale in Belgium and Luis Solana of Spain. Apparently for the benefit of Miguel Canalejo and Marquez Balin, Solana preened about this advance knowledge of the transaction. I thought, "Fine, as long as he supports the joint venture." Solana was mercurial, so until the money was paid, I knew there would be ups and downs. There were. Solana wanted Roxane, but he also wanted some special privileges with her that were not accorded to other investors. He would not, therefore, be easy to satisfy.

21

Paris Politics

A wise man once remarked that life is never simple in love and in war. He might have added "in business" as well. Negotiations, especially with sovereign governments, are full of booby traps, bureaucratic snafus, and back-alley politics. In fact, it was just for some of these reasons that ITT wanted to reduce its worldwide exposure to perpetual uncertainties. The point was driven home shortly after my return to Cap d'Antibes from Madrid, when Michel David-Weill called to say he had received extremely disquieting news from Paris. The new French Government, which was evaluating the appointment or reappointment of the heads of all of the government-owned major industries, including CGE, was indicating serious reservations about reappointing Georges Pebereau.

When Minister Baladur had requested a deadline extension to July 31, I felt all the odds were in favor of approval of the agreement. Press reaction in France was favorable—proclaiming a coup for France in the worldwide telecommunications race. Disapproval could bring great political criticism, "lack-of-courage" headlines, statements that France would "miss the opportunity of the century." I figured the Government could come up with the required funds, but it never occurred to me that Minister Baladur did not want to reappoint Georges Pebereau as chairman of CGE. Such a move would be a misstep that could undo Roxane, with a new man saying she was too rich or that he needed time to renegotiate her terms, which would mean no deal.

Stories had it that the French Government felt pressured by Pebereau's deal with ITT; that Georges had manipulated them; that he had not provided them with sufficient information before initialing the deal. Further, there were rumblings that a substantial cash infusion into CGE would be required to make the transaction financially sound—as much as $750 million.

Other stories indicated that Pebereau was not on the best of terms with RPR, the Chirac party, because of his loyal service as an industrial leader under the socialist government. Whatever the stories, they were upsetting. All of the work thus far had been the joint vision of myself and Georges Pebereau: I felt it would be extremely difficult for anyone else to accept the vision that we had developed. I could not conceive that it could be someone who worked for the indomitable Pebereau in CGE.

Names of potential industrial leaders to replace Pebereau were bandied about Paris. It seemed that the size of the deal and the attitude of the French Government were such that it would be easy for the new individual to back away. All the work of the previous fifteen months would be lost, but, most important, a great future for the joint venture and for our ITT companies would also be lost. Finally, I feared a terrific backlash—a drop in the value of ITT stock. Our balance sheet would not receive the boost we had anticipated, and the overseas exposures of the corporation would be even more celebrated than before the deal became public.

Sunday morning, July 20, Michel David-Weill called me at my Cap d'Antibes hotel and asked me to come to his house, Sous-le-Vent, at 4 P.M. Georges Pebereau was en route to the south of France with news that he felt was critically important. I said, "Of course," and Pebereau arrived shortly after I did. Dressed in sports attire, he seemed somewhat in disarray. He spoke rapidly in French to Michel, and even in English he spoke in a staccato. He was obviously agitated.

Georges indicated that he did not know what was going on with respect to his reappointment. He had heard the rumors that others were hearing, but whether or not he was reappointed, he wanted the joint venture to go through. He felt it was right for CGE, right for France and for ITT. In order for the deal to go forward, he said that ITT would have to make two commitments to the French Government. As he talked, I recalled that his car was parked outside when Michel and I had left the palace of the Minister of Finance the night of Thursday, June 26.

I did not know it at the time, but Minister Baladur had been asked to put 5 billion French francs (more than $700 million) into CGE in order to provide a balance sheet that would allow the joint venture to go forward. This, perhaps, was the most significant cause of the Government's irritation with Pebereau—that the sum had not been specified in advance as necessary for the deal. In view of this, Baladur obviously had asked—either directly then of Pebereau or through Minister Madelin—for two concessions from ITT. The first was that we would raise no objection to CGE's CIT Alcatel's forming a joint venture with AT&T in the field of telecommunications transmission. If the AT&T-Alcatel transmission agreement were signed, presumably the French Government would give AT&T the 16 percent market share previously held in France by CGCT, the former French subsidiary that ITT had given up in 1982. I remembered that Georges Pebereau had told me AT&T was about to get this 16 percent in the spring of 1985, and then in the fall of 1985, and it still had not been awarded.

Answering Pebereau, with Michel listening, I insisted that ITT would never agree to the AT&T joint venture. That would cancel the deal. The ITT system had strong transmission capabilities—at BTM, FACE, Standard Electrica, and Standard Electrik Lorenz— and there was no way we could surrender that business to competition with another Alcatel joint venture. The two were not compatible. If Alcatel controlled the total activity, it then would favor the Alcatel-AT&T joint venture over the ITT system transmission capabilities. I indicated it would be untenable to our system house managers.

Pebereau said, "Okay," and he raised his hands and exclaimed, "I am telling you that is going to be one condition and you will have to decide what to do. I cannot tell you what to do, but it will be a necessary condition."

Rather disgustedly I said, "Georges, what's the other?" And he replied, "The other condition is that while it is okay for you to have 30 percent of the joint venture, the French Government is unwilling to have CGE entirely responsible for bringing in the other partners. ITT must take responsibility for bringing in another partner acceptable to CGE for 7 percent of the total joint venture, at $300 million minimum investment. The new investor would pay the same as Société Générale and CTNE in Spain as they come into the joint venture."

I responded, "Georges, you and I agreed in the beginning that CGE had to buy it all and then be responsible for any resale. CGE had to be the one to redistribute the shares or ITT would not be assured of getting the total price we wanted. I told you at the beginning that if we sold you 51 percent, and we kept 30 percent, and we were responsible for selling any part of the difference between 81 percent and 100 percent, that we would not be able to get an equivalent price. People would hold us up, and that is why I said it had to be all done by CGE. I stand with that. I will not yield."

Pebereau said, "Okay. I'm only telling you these are the two conditions. You can think about them some more."

I replied, "I'm not going to think about them at all. I've held the line from the very beginning on the things that were absolutely essential to ITT, to its board, and to its shareholders, and you can let the French Government know that I will yield on neither of those points."

Georges again raised his hands, saying, "Okay, Rand, I told

you. Either you want this or you don't. These are two conditions that have to be met, and if they can't be met, that's it.''

Sensing the tension between the two of us, Michel stepped in and became a calming catalyst. There had to be significant added tension for Pebereau, since he still had no idea what would happen to him. The rumors swirling around him in Paris and in the international press must have been rather insulting and discouraging. Yet, here he was, still trying to keep Roxane alive whether or not he was the one to have her.

The rumors, in fact, had become much more specific. An article in one of the French daily newspapers identified Pierre Suard as the likely replacement for Georges Pebereau. Suard was described as a close friend of Baladur and Chirac, a member of the party. As the head of CGE's CIT Alcatel, Suard had participated in our negotiations, but I had met him only once during negotiations and two or three times socially. He had seemed extremely negative about Roxane because of his concern for the deteriorating situation in Spain. In that one particular meeting, which had occurred in June, he had been intransigent that Spain represented too great a business risk.

After that meeting in which Pebereau had brought in Suard, Georges told me, "Look, Rand, I wanted you to see what my people are like. There is no unanimity here. I have people who are very difficult in this deal, and that is why I am being as tough as I am on certain points in the negotiations.''

I told him, "Georges, I have the same situation as you do. I have another company in the wings that certain of our people favor. You are well aware of that and I am the one with our board who is trying to drive this thing through just as you are.''

Georges responded, "Rand, I know that. We are partners.''

Now, at Sous-le-Vent, surrounded by exquisite paintings as the evening sea air blew through the great house, Georges for the first time seemed almost pathetic. He said, "Rand, we have become friends. No matter what happens to me, don't let our agreement fail. You can work things out later, but don't destroy the deal.'' Michel and I saw him to the door. There wasn't much more for Michel and me to discuss, so I left too.

The following Tuesday, I had lunch with Georges Pebereau at CGE headquarters in Paris. Without rancor, without dismay, without criticism of the Government, without any sign of lack of patriotism, with no recrimination, he told me that he was not being reappointed chairman of CGE. The French Government had decided on Pierre Suard. Georges fully supported their decision, because Pierre had worked for him for many years. He had great confidence in Suard and was certain that Pierre would support the CGE/ITT deal. The next day, the appointments of the new managing directors and chairmen of the French companies were announced. There were gala parties in Paris honoring the new appointments, and one of the most celebrated appointees was Pierre Suard. It was now imperative that I meet with Suard to see whether it was possible to salvage our negotiations, which appeared headed for imminent collapse. The conditions, as stated by Pebereau, were impossible, but I was cautiously optimistic.

Suard was waiting for me in the same conference room in which Georges Pebereau and I had met at least fifteen times. I began to think he would indeed decide to go forward: To decide otherwise would have indicated excessive caution, would have subjected him to considerable criticism from the French press for being afraid of "the deal of the century"—the biggest alliance among European industries since the European Economic Community had been formed. I felt that Baladur and Chirac would also find it difficult to let this opportunity pass. Nevertheless, my greatest concern was that Suard would ask for another extension. I had already made it clear there could be none, but I had seen enough to know it could be requested again. I would simply say, "I have made up my mind. Pierre, you have been in this long enough. There will be no extension. You have to decide."

Suard, a careful dresser, good looking, was confident in English and impressive in French. After the initial congratulations, he began our conversation with a discussion of the two French Government conditions that Georges Pebereau had introduced when we had met at Michel David-Weill's home. Pebereau had been agitated then, and perhaps I had not asked him enough questions.

The first condition I was being asked to approve by Pierre Suard was perfectly acceptable to ITT. The joint venture with AT&T in transmission would be an arm of ITT/CGE's joint venture, so it would not be in competition with the system houses of ITT. Furthermore, the agreement contemplated having AT&T discontinue all transmission equipment development and manufacture in the United States. Instead, this responsibility would be handled by Alcatel in France and certain Alcatel facilities in the United States. This was an acceptable arrangement that in fact would increase the transmission market share of the ITT/CGE joint venture. So it was very easy for me to say, "Pierre, I did not fully understand the AT&T deal as Georges Pebereau explained it. I understand it now, and it's all right."

Pierre continued, "Okay, then there is a second condition. The French Government insists that you be responsible for your 30 percent plus 7 percent more of the joint venture."

I replied, "Pierre, I already indicated we will not be responsible for 30 percent with a guarantee to sell an additional 7 percent. We would be perfectly happy to take and keep 37 percent, with you buying 63 percent. Then we could decide to sell that 7 percent or not to sell it as we might jointly agree in the future. I would be satisfied to keep 37 percent just for ITT and reduce the cash amount to be paid to ITT from $1.8 billion to $1.5 billion."

Pierre said, "So, we are in agreement. I will support the deal, and I feel quite confident the French Government will approve it and that the Board of Directors of CGE will approve it early next week."

That was it. I got up, we shook hands. I told him, "Pierre, this is going to be a great development. I am pleased you have the courage to step up to this. I am also pleased that you have been part of the negotiations, so you know what we are doing. We will work closely with you to achieve a final closing by the end of December 1986, which is extremely important, I know, to both of us. You need to achieve that date for your financial closing and privatization program, and we need it to avoid detrimental tax changes in the United States.''

He said, "I understand that. We should probably target to complete things, if the French Government approves, by the end of November to be sure we make that December date.''

I replied, "Fine. I'll have people come here and we will get rolling immediately.''

I departed for the United States. Roxane was approved. The newspapers were full of the news, and on Tuesday, July 29, I returned to Paris again. We wrapped up the deal in the next two days and formed the negotiating teams to complete the final package. All major matters had been concluded, but we knew there would be new situations we had not contemplated. I was quite certain, because of my great confidence in Howard Aibel and the attractiveness of Roxane to CGE, that we would be able to wrap her up by the end of the year. We had to.

Our dealings with the French Government were always difficult, since it was never totally clear whether the agenda was dominated by political considerations or economic ones or both. Perhaps it was the confirmation of the two factors that made it so frustrating at times but that also led to the eventual success.

22

Covering All the Bases

W ho would have dreamed in 1980 that seven years later, ITT would be divesting majority ownership in telecommunications—the division Harold Geneen had described as the company's heartline when he hired me. After the public disclosure of the joint venture, I called Harold Geneen to fill him in on what we had done. His immediate reaction was, "Rand, you are doing the right thing. The situation has changed in Europe. This has been coming on slowly for some time. I congratulate you. I think you have things in order over there."

The only time that Geneen had not been supportive of my efforts was when the dividend was cut in 1984. I could not breathe a word of it to him in advance, and it caught him by surprise. Throughout his career as chief executive officer, he had pursued a corporate philosophy of continually improving dividends, and from what he knew about the balance sheet of ITT, he felt the cut was unnecessary. His immediate reaction was negative and at first he was even openly critical to a couple of people, but then he stopped that, in deference to ITT and me. As time went on, however, I think Harold came to realize that the dividend reduction was needed.

My basic dedication is to the company that Harold Geneen and Sosthenes Behn put together. I feel strongly that their strategy was correct and that it was a strategy for the century. ITT has not changed radically. It is a service company of substantial proportions as well as a manufacturing company. New equipment industries have been added: automotive, electronic components, fluid technology, and defense technology. In addition, significant service industries, different from those in telecommunications, have been developed and incorporated into the company: insurance, both casualty and life; financial services; hotels; communications business services. Sosthenes Behn would not feel uncomfortable with ITT's current image.

Nevertheless, the company is now far different in structure and management techniques from when Harold Geneen left. The focus is sharper. Many of the top-heavy staff jobs are gone, so there is limited second-guessing of line managers. In the old days, about 140 executives attended huge general management meetings. Today, there may be twenty. The company no longer thinks of itself as a clever street fighter in the corporate jungle, but rather as an ethical force in business.

I believe that the most important characteristic of a business executive is integrity. It is also the most important tenet to teach your children—to strive for truth, telling the truth and never being afraid of it. As a result, you do not do things that cause you to lie or make you feel you have to lie.

It may be hard to reverse the ethical slide that has taken place in the United States in the last decade or so. No court decision will change that. Within the highest ranks of the Reagan administration, more than 110 officials appointed to federal posts have been accused of ethical misconduct, and six special prosecutors were fully employed to investigate corruption and other forms of sleazy behavior. But these unethical government officials are not the only ones on the take. Private greed is just as rampant, perhaps more so, although it is often passed off in the name of "business." Activities that were considered to be in the gutter are now up on the sidewalks of America.

A number of aggressive businessmen have pursued dubious practices that skirt the edge of propriety, if not legality—price fixing, cronyism, golden parachutes. No amount of ethics courses at business schools will suffice for tomorrow's managers if they have no moral anchor when they arrive, and if "enrich thyself" is the chief motto of society. And almost as deadly for business is an attitude that encourages watching your own derrière, being fearful of being innovative. Too many American corporations are suffering from this problem. Perhaps it is only human nature, but the merger-and-acquisition trend may, for all the learned and self-serving comment to the contrary, be counterproductive. Companies cannot be acquired and cast off without great cost. "Corporations," as Felix Rohatyn has noted, "are not Erector sets."

A short time after our agreement in France, a letter from Jay Pritzker arrived at my home with the following message: "Congratulations, Rand. If I had known you were going to bite the bullet on telecommunications, I would have held on to my stock. C'est la vie. Jay."

I wrote to thank him, but I could not help recalling sitting in his Hyatt Hotel office on August 10, 1984, when he told me that life was just a game. My feelings about Jay Pritzker bordered on deep resentment. The Pritzker family fortune had been built by Jay's father in Chicago, and Jay had known nothing but great wealth. I had grown up on a Minnesota farm in the Depression days. I left that farm as a young teenager in the middle of World War II. I later went to West Point because I was excited about it, but it also relieved the financial burden on my family—three children were in college at the same time. I worked my way up the hard way, through government, Honeywell, and ITT, and I resented the idea that a guy with inherited money could walk in and destroy the career I had built—and do it with nonchalance and indifference. Perhaps for Pritzker it *was* nothing but a game, but my family was no game to me. It was serious business, and I resented Pritzker's intrusion into my life.

Moreover, the many companies that Pritzker had purchased for less than they were worth, by the methods at his disposal, made him no credit to American business. Naturally, I wondered how he got away with what he did. Even with his much-touted philanthropic activities, I could only think of a John Steinbeck line about "some of the wolfish financiers who spent two-thirds of their lives clawing fortunes out of the guts of society, and the latter third pushing it back"—and, I might add, with their names engraved on the returns.

Shortly thereafter, Jessie and I ran into our other nemesis, Irwin Jacobs, at a dinner dance hosted by Drexel Burnham at the Metropolitan Museum of Art. It looked like a duplicate of the West Coast "Pirates Party," with an array of the brokerage house's junk-bond customers. While I found Fred Joseph personally charming, I have grave doubts about his company's role in the leveraging of America and financing the raiders. As we were turning a gallery corner, Jessie whispered, "Hey, Rand, should we turn around? There's 'The Three Rs.'" Once upon a time, I had accused Irwin, recorded in the "Heard on the Street" column of the *Wall Street Journal,* of practicing the three Rs: "Run down the management, run up the stock, and run away with the money."

I said, "No, let's say hello. We might as well cover all the bases."

We did, and we talked about Minnesota's Lake Minnetonka, about Irwin's new boat works, which he bought because he wanted better care for his yacht. We talked amiably enough and I reflected that if he had not tried to mess around with my company, I might have liked him.

The next evening, Pierre Suard and several of his key associates joined ITT top management for dinner at the River Club on New York's East River. It was an effort on our part to ensure that, during the period of final closing, we maintained good relations at the top. Pierre and I both wanted to correct problems quickly if they could not be resolved by our people. The evening was enjoyable, with speeches by both the French and the American contingents. We were off to a good start with all the people who would be participating on the management and negotiating sides of both organizations.

The next day, during a private luncheon with Pierre Suard, we summarized what had to be done in the next two months. We agreed that my most important task was to see that System 12 continued on its strong upward curve. System 12 was on a roll. Press criticism of the system had subsided, and ITT Europe headquarters personnel were confident we would deliver more System 12 switching lines around the world than would be delivered by any other supplier, including AT&T, in that time period.

Spain had become our joint task, or was it our common cross? Luis Solana was taking different positions in the press every other day, creating a good deal of confusion about Spanish interest in investing in the joint venture. And there was still no resolution of a plan for ITT's Standard Electrica to retire, furlough, or discharge the 5,000 or so excess laborers whom the company was bringing to work, feeding lunch, and busing home.

Spain, with a socialist government, was doing just as previous Spanish governments had done—giving the unions what the unions thought was their due, despite severe setbacks to the Spanish economy. This contrasted sharply with the approach Italy had taken some years earlier, when it had been locked in labor battles. Its economy was at a standstill, with troubles in every industry from Fiat to Italtel. But Italian industrialists such as Agnelli and Pirelli, with the necessary support of the Government, had loosened the grip of the unions. The extraneous labor force was released from the factories, including unnecessary management layers. The ensuing rejuvenation of Italian industry placed Italy at the front rank of growth economies by 1986. On the other hand, Spain continued to be locked into the statist, welfare principles of Generalissimo Francisco Franco, who maintained that a job was a job for life, whether or not it was productive. This caused most industries to operate inefficiently. Spanish officials loved to talk about high-tech exports, but it was mostly talk.

New industries in Spain were passively subsidized by not being required to accept the labor commitments of existing industries. This penalized the companies that had suffered the longest under the tolerated and unprofitable conditions. Seemingly no one, not even Prime Minister Felipe Gonzalez—who, together with the business community, could alter events—was prepared to go to the mat with the unions, to make the changes that could get Spain on the track that Italy had already traveled. Pierre Suard and I recognized Spain and Standard Electrica as, perhaps, the most significant challenge to be overcome for the long-term health and stability of the joint venture. Fortunately for us, Spain is now changing, showing signs of becoming a new economic power in Europe. It stands to benefit greatly from the total integration of the European Economic Community in 1992. And the new Alcatel has reached a sound agreement there.

The following day, in Washington, I described the joint venture to top executives of the Department of Defense, whom Howard Aibel had notified prior to the July 1986 signature. We had wanted no quick rebuff, and, of course, our U.S. defense companies were not included in the transaction; they would remain exclusively within ITT.

Shortly afterward, I held meetings with Lord Keith, chairman of the board of STC in London. (Roxane included most of our 24 percent ownership in Standard Telephones and Cables of the United Kingdom.) I wanted to meet with Lord Keith to ensure his support in effecting the transaction so that these shares—which at the time were worth about $225 million—could be included in ITT's contribution to the joint venture. The transfer probably had to be approved by the Home Office of the British Ministry of Industry. Lord Keith was lukewarm to the transaction, at best, but I did not feel he would lobby to stop it.

Meanwhile, terrorist murders of executives on Paris streets had created a siege-type environment, and CGE security was tight. At its entrance was a gate that descended after each car entered. The car then approached another gate, which opened after the first gate closed, allowing entrance to the CGE courtyard. Pierre and I spent three hours resolving certain issues that had arisen in the course of negotiations. He received my endorsement to add Cables de Lyons, the CGE cable company, to Roxane, at a price to be agreed upon. It would make Roxane the largest cable company in the world, but would reduce ITT's ownership in the joint venture to between 34 and 35 percent.

At Victoria House in Brussels, we held the European telecommunications meeting and dinner with all of the system house managers. We discussed Roxane in exquisite detail. Each managing director reported his opinions of how the joint-venture idea was being accepted in his country, and all reports were favorable. Each country wanted assurance, however, that there would be no change in System 12. Pierre Suard was most helpful in signing letters to this effect, letters complimentary of System 12. We indeed were covering all the bases.

Upon returning to the United States, I attended a dinner for Giuglio Andreotti, the Italian foreign minister, at American Express headquarters on Wall Street. To my great surprise, Andreotti, despite all of our attention to Italian concern, was unaware of the fact that ITT had retained a 37 percent interest in the joint venture and therefore would stay close to our Italian company, FACE. Assuming we were getting out of telecommunications and FACE entirely, he was extremely interested to know about the major position we were maintaining. I told him I would be chairman of the supervisory board of the new company for at least three years.

As a top member of the cabinet of the Government of Italy, Andreotti's understanding of ITT's role in the joint venture was important. It was evident that high-level people in Italy were purposely confusing our role in the joint venture to suit their own purposes. I was thinking particularly of Marisa Bellisario, the head of Italtel, the government-owned telephone equipment company. I advised Pierre Suard of this, so that his communications channels could assist in strengthening the message about ITT's continued presence.

Felix Rohatyn and I reviewed the French situation, particularly the new policies of Jacques Chirac, to ensure that we continued in the French Government's good graces. Felix was quoted in the American press about his dismay with what was going on in the investment banking community, the legal community supporting the investment banking community, and in the corporate raider community. He was very concerned about a significant backlash, because there were implications that what had been going on, in his view, demonstrated a level of greed that might not stop short of illegal actions.

I commented to Felix that what was being heralded as deregulation of the marketplace was, in reality, an unwillingness to govern. Felix was unhappy with current trends, though Lazard Frères was no doubt profiting from it. His concern was that unbridled greed might well bring down the whole house of cards.

Perhaps the natural consequence of financial deregulation, under President Reagan, was to release rigidified industries from the heavy hand of government. Most businesspeople, especially those in large corporations, were solidly behind the efforts to deregulate, to let in the sunlight of competition—or so we thought. At first, it appeared to have real value. In the heretofore-regulated industries—utilities, trucking, airlines, banking—competition did lead to lower prices, consolidation and/or bankruptcy of inefficient companies, and a field day for business mergers and acquisitions and raiders. The I-love-business administration turned its back on enforcement, whether it was in the SEC or the antitrust division of the Justice Department. Regulatory guidelines were overrun by aggressive and ruthless financiers who were indifferent to their social consequences and had no fear of government's chastisement. And our celebratory society made culture pop heroes of men whose lasting contribution was to enrich themselves by shuffling corporate assets. The philosopher who cautioned us to be careful of what we wished for, lest we get it, became the symbol of eight years of economic laissez-faire. Unwittingly, we have produced a weakened economy, reduced international standing, and a weakened corporate America.

Enlightened business circles are slowly realizing that some regulation is not necessarily a bad thing, that government has a role to play not only in separating contending interests, but also in protecting citizens from rapacious conduct. Unhappily, the Reagan administration's assumption that the act of freeing up business would be adequate to stimulate the business environment and social welfare was wide of the mark. The net results have been to encourage cutting corners, enthrone greed, and raise financial chicanery. These are not admirable bequests.

Fortunately, a major countervailing force is the publicly held corporation, whose greatest virtue is perhaps its openness. Publicly held corporations must operate openly and are subject to public pressures, far more so than privately held corporations. If they produce a bad product, the word is out, and their market prices can drop significantly. Such is the discipline of the market. Privately held corporations can taken internal steps that are strictly in the interest of the owners, not in the public interest.

Public controls on publicly held corporations—from the Securities and Exchange Commission, the Federal Trade Commission, and the stock exchanges—are significantly greater than for privately held corporations. Furthermore, the activities of publicly held corporations are completely open to inquiries and press scrutiny. Several business magazines, newspapers, and TV programs derive their living from following publicly held corporations.

It is good for America that young men and women are climbing the corporate ladder. This capability produces a sense of mission, leads to quality products and services, and instills a sense of responsibility to the public, the press, local communities, and share-owners. After a lifetime in public corporations, I am convinced that workers and their managers develop a sense of self-respect for the public and its needs. Unfortunately, too few critics look at public corporations from this vantage point, and almost no one writes about them in a complimentary way. But they indeed provide an avenue for advancement for the youth of America who wish to compete, perform, and contribute.

The chief executive of a public corporation faces a variety of challenges in ethics, morals, and even in legalities that may produce far greater pressures than exist for the owner of a private company. Certain people claim that they want to go private to avoid public reporting and to be able to run their business for the long term without having to meet quarterly income and dividend requirements. That, however, does not make them better corporations. While there are privately held corporations that produce very high-quality goods and services, they do not cast dark shadows on those that are publicly held.

Another aspect of the large public corporation is only now being appreciated—entrepreneurship, which provides continuity through the whole industrial process. The ability of Americans to fulfill their dreams by starting a new and innovative business has been touted in the 1980s as the answer to everything—from employing the unemployable to the one sure method of self-enrichment. And, in truth, small businesses were responsible for most of the employment growth in the eighties. They were, and continue to be, a source of creative ideas and some breakthrough technology, but it should be remembered that most of their entrepreneurs received their background experience in publicly held corporations. From California's Silicon Valley to Massachusetts's Route 128, nearly a thousand electronics manufacturers have sprung up. While many are profitable, many more are not. Furthermore, the game of musical chairs among their research-and-development staffs has lent no stability to the scene. One critic, Professor Charles H. Ferguson of MIT, has warned of the dangers of "chronic entrepreneurialism."

Small entrepreneurial companies have an exceedingly difficult time reaching a critical mass, of being competitive in the international market where we all must play. Small companies—however flexible, adaptable, brilliant, and innovative—are no match for the fifteen or twenty huge Japanese multinationals when their singular product line reaches a mature stage. Large, vertically integrated companies are best at exploiting mass-produced items such as semiconductors, whereas small entrepreneurial companies may be best at developing the elusive superconductor. America's large public corporations must do more to entice creative research-and-development personnel, and, just as important, learn better ways to exploit that technology, even if it means a lack of short-term profit. American companies must insist on continuity from the drawing boards to the sales counters: They can do that only by constantly upgrading the value of their labor forces and lengthening their financial horizons.

Pension funds used to be concerned with long-term fiduciary responsibilities. Unfortunately, many have jettisoned that attitude and have myopically shortened their horizons. The pension funds have played a key role in the takeover game. Pension funds are now among the largest holders of equity in the institutional pie. Estimates suggest that institutions will hold half of all equity by the turn of the century. Pension funds mandated by the Employee Retirement Income Security Act (ERISA) already manage $1.5 trillion. They are as trendy as the latest boutiques, adopting the latest portfolio management techniques, whether they be portfolio insurance schemes or index arbitrage. From post-1987-Crash obituaries, it is obvious that these institutional funds were to some degree responsible for the volatility of the market. Their fiduciary responsibility has not always been exercised with great caution. Some pension funds have been substantial buyers of junk bonds to raise their yields by a few percentage points. Inadvertently or not, they have made hostile takeovers easier to accomplish, again destabilizing the financial world.

In the United Kingdom, the Bank of England performs an oversight function when there is a problem between the equity owners and management. This tends to short-circuit hostile proxy wars. Working with institutional representatives, the bank has been instrumental in making the institutional investors' views known to the Boards of Directors. A similar procedure might be adopted in the United States to reduce friction between owners and managers.

It may be time for socially responsible pension funds to look beyond return on investment. "What price return?" is not an idle question. Perhaps pension-fund portfolio managers should be judged on other criteria as well. There are ways to employ their funds in a more direct fashion—conscious of their required returns, but not governed solely by portfolio performance in the market. Some half-dozen pension funds already are involved in sponsoring community housing projects. This form of social investment need not run counter to the Prudent Man rule as long as institutions can get a reasonable return on their funds. Critics may assert that it is not the function of pension funds to rebuild America. If we do not want the government to do it, perhaps this is an idea whose time has come. Such investment not only would be socially constructive, it would also remove some of the pressure to perform only in terms of the stock market. Finally, it would also remove some of the pension fund money from the pool of assets that raiders now have access to (and frequently plunder) when they are successful in a takeover raid against a publicly held company.

Meanwhile, two publicly held corporations, ITT and CGE, separated by an ocean, were readying to pass the baton for the final lap of the race to consummate Roxane.

23

The Finish Line

T he race to cross the finish line was a deadly serious one, one ITT could ill afford to lose. Plenty of things still could go wrong in the rush to deliverance. Delay would have caused legal problems, but those were minor compared to the potential tax liabilities if it dragged on beyond December 31, 1986. The Tax Reform Act of 1986 would come into force on January 1, 1987, and the revised code would assess a heavy burden for our tardiness. If we failed to finalize all the multifaceted aspects of these global negotiations before the new tax law, ITT would lose $288 million in cash, almost $2 per share. That would have a devastating effect on our earnings, which in turn would damage the price of our stock, and possibly bring the raiders back to cause further mischief. Worse, it would have obscured and confused the whole purpose of Roxane. It was imperative to complete the legalities on time.

It was equally important to smooth the transition if the new joint venture was to get off to a good start. To build confidence, we wanted to be totally open—with our books, our systems, our management, and in many respects with the hearts and minds of all the people involved. A genuine admiration was developing between CGE and ITT. Initially, there had been some friction, doubts, and

214

questions of credibility. All that was disappearing slowly but surely, and a team effort was becoming evident. Many ITT executives had not thought that possible.

Pierre Suard, Chema Fernandez from INDETEL (a major supplier to Telmex) in Mexico, plus Gerhard Zeidler and Jo Cornu from Brussels, met with me in New York on Monday, October 20, 1986, concerning the Mexican System 12 situation. Progress was being made, but the purpose of this meeting was to reinforce priorities: the significance of maintaining our System 12 performance through the closing of the joint venture and the initial performance of the joint venture in 1987 and thereafter. At ITT's Bolton Conference Center, Pierre Suard spoke informally after dinner to the management team, which included our system house managing directors from Europe. He delivered a speech of welcome, another step in building confidence. It would still be a couple of months before the door would close and Roxane would have a legal name and address in Holland.

The next morning, Pierre presented a formal summary of CGE and the new joint venture, going into fine detail and speaking with a mixture of humor and firmness. He did a good job of presenting the new business to the rest of ITT, and he realized that the rest of ITT's management had increased enthusiasm about the ITT minority position in the joint venture.

These complicated transactions, plus the necessity of seeking approval from numerous governments in order to execute transfers of ownership, illuminated the problems a takeover raider would have had in coping with ITT: Evidently Jay Pritzker had partly realized this in his efforts to enlist a "blue-ribbon board" and the cooperation of people such as Georges Pebereau, Lord Weinstock, and Dr. Karlheinz Kaske. Even a friendly environment had any number of potential pitfalls. In the course of the past several months, reminders of raider activity had left the halls of ITT, but the press was still active in describing the situation surrounding other companies.

The *Wall Street Journal* printed an effective and fair representation of the position of the Business Roundtable on raiders, unfriendly takeovers, greenmail, and all of the associated aberrations of these activities. Andy Sigler, the principal spokesman for the Business Roundtable on mergers and acquisitions, had met with the *Journal* editors and had corrected some of the impressions the editors had gained from the engaging but misleading Boone Pickens, who had met with them previously.

On Wednesday, November 12, at a Business Roundtable policy committee meeting, the chairman, Roger Smith of GM, asked Andy Sigler to brief the Business Roundtable. Andy stressed that the business community would have to be more open and aggressive in presenting its side. The raiders had been getting all the favorable publicity from a press that appeared to enjoy hounding established firms. As a result, the raiders were receiving more public sympathy than their victims.

In general, businesspeople are reluctant to speak their minds in matters that are near to them and of which they have some special knowledge. This is a tragedy for the country, since it deprives us of much accumulated wisdom and some special insights into many of our contemporary problems. Or, to put it another way, I am concerned that businesspeople, and particularly some who run the largest corporations, are not given the opportunity to express their opinions. Indeed, they are not expected to voice their thoughts on such socially significant matters as abortion and AIDS. Writers are perfectly acceptable commentators, as are newspaper editors, theater actors, movie stars, and even takeover artists.

I flew from Hartford to Morristown, New Jersey, after the Hartford Fire Insurance board meeting on Friday, November 15. We were spending the weekend in Smoke Rise. The phone rang. Then Jessie said, "Turn on the TV. There is big news, they caught Boesky." Ivan Boesky's name was all too familiar to Jessie. I turned on the TV and the news was spilling out. Dennis Levine, an insider-trading violator charged earlier, had named names, and a big one was falling. What had to happen, happened. I remember thinking that maybe this nonsense would cease. It was the beginning of the nightmare Wall Street had been building up to since the Bronfmans went after Conoco in the early 1980s. I had no pity. I only hoped that ultimately the SEC would get them all.

Near the end of November 1986, ITT had its final general management meetings in Brussels. There was some nostalgia, but our efforts were bent on ensuring that we would meet our budget for 1986 and that the plans for 1987 were in good shape. Pierre Suard was obliged to cancel his appearance at dinner in the evening, so the affair was an ITT swan song. Pierre also missed the next morning's session because he was attending the funeral of the chairman of Renault, Mr. Pierre Besse, who had been assassinated by terrorists a few days earlier. We had arranged that Pierre would arrive in time for lunch with Howard Aibel, John Chluski, and myself. After lunch, Suard would take over a series of private one-on-one meetings with each of the managing directors. He intended to lay the groundwork for a specific change of control.

Prior to my departure from Brussels for New York, Pierre and I met with our two public relations executives, Juan Cappello and Françoise Sampermans, to arrange the program for a joint press conference in early January in Brussels, after the final closing on Roxane. Howard Aibel had done an outstanding job conducting the incredibly complex legal negotiations; Juan Cappello was doing an equally creative job in developing a joint public relations program. We had gone from a time when people thought ITT was getting out of telecommunications to a new era when ITT was organizing its major stake in the financing, policies, and operation of the joint venture.

At an end-of-the-year Trilateral Commission reception for Clayton Yeutter, the U.S. trade representative, I confided to him that one of the reasons ITT had made the transaction with CGE was that the trade activities of the U.S. Government were making it almost impossible for us to continue in Europe. The Government was treating ITT like a European firm, giving the company no credit for its vast European activities, which brought dividends to the United States. ITT's balance of payments was unusually positive in the direction of the United States. Our companies in Europe, owned by U.S. shareholders, were being treated as European. Companies such as AT&T and Northern Telecom received government support to move in to take our market share in Europe.

On the other hand, in the United States we were not given opportunities or benefits for those American-owned European companies. In fact, they had to compete on the same basis as any other European company. Nevertheless, we were being set up by our European competitors, who called our European subsidiaries "American" companies. We had the worst of both worlds and were caught in the middle. We were hit by Clayton Yeutter and Bruce Smart, people in the State Department and Commerce Department, on the one hand, as being European, and we were hit by our competitors and some of our European customers as being American, on the other hand. Yeutter seemed somewhat startled by my comments, but I did not feel he would lose any sleep over them.

The United States has been rather backward, compared to other industrialized and newly industrialized countries, at exporting its wares. Part of that was because it was easier to "export" to Lima, Ohio, than Lima, Peru. Unlike resource-limited societies like the United Kingdom and Japan, Switzerland and Israel, we had the resources and the consumers for a continental economy. Only recently have we become export-conscious—to some degree because of our rapidly growing trade imbalances. But the Carter and Reagan administrations never took our export markets seriously enough. They used embargo diplomacy or settled for benign neglect in lieu of a real policy. After a fivefold growth in the U.S. trade deficit between 1980 and 1987, the major governmental response was to lower the value of our currency. Efforts at righting the trade deficits with Japan have been pitiful—we spoke softly and carried a small stick. Neither one did us much good. The least little counterpressures for fairer trade were immediately opposed by the Japanese (and Korean) lobby in Washington, with their hired flaks and legal mouthpieces. The Japanese have spent enormous sums to protect their positions, far more money in their lobbying efforts than the Business Roundtable.

America should wake up to the free ride the Japanese have had in our markets and the difficulties we have had in theirs. They are slowly retreating from their tribal mercantilism, but the surpluses of cash they have accumulated have placed the Japanese banking system in a dominant world role.

The Japanese must accept some blame for avoiding global responsibilities and world leadership—*The Economist* magazine once remarked that "Japan seldom thinks about anything but money." They view the world in the most narrow commercial sense: Did they offer to pay any of the costs in patrolling the Persian Gulf, even though 60 percent of the oil was destined for their homeland? Have they taken the lead in Third World loans or famine relief? What is their stand on apartheid, other than to buy up the assets American companies have abandoned? However, corporate America must also bear some responsibility for giving the Japanese every opportunity to capture markets by default. From radios and transistors to computers and semiconductors, household appliances to motor vehicles, American producers withdrew from the marketplace. The reasons were always the same: There was no quick money in the audio disc or the videocassette recorder, the small car, the portable washing machine. This myopic view was not shared by other countries, which did a far better job encouraging cooperation among domestic manufacturers and protecting their workers and their markets.

When the Japanese tried to market VCRs in France, the French Government wisely restricted their imports—they had to pass through Poitiers, where there was only one customs official avail-

able to inspect imports. When the Japanese banned French surf-
boards because they were not "safe" for Japanese consumers, the
French suggested that they might have to review France's open
borders to Japanese motorcycles, since they might not be "safe"
for French consumers. The Japanese quickly got the message.

The Reagan administration was, for lack of a better description,
distracted in defending American commercial interests. In world
politics you can be loved or respected—Americans have a genetic
weakness that makes them wish only to be loved. It is no wonder
that our trade position remains weak and the dollar 40 percent
below its 1980 value. Nor is it simply a politically partisan weakness. Senator Edward Kennedy once remarked to me that it was
fine if the Japanese bought our assets, for then they would be part
of the problem.

As the closing date approached, we learned that the German
cartel office had approved the joint venture, and the approval papers were moving rapidly in Spain and Norway. Everything was
on target, but in business you can never be sure—things can never
go too well. We were still having trouble transferring the shares
representing 24 percent ownership of STC. STC did not want them
transferred, and suddenly CGE was acting as if it did not want the
STC shares. Ever since Cables de Lyons had been added to the
joint venture, CGE had worried about competition in undersea cable competitions with STC. Howard Aibel went to Paris to negotiate an agreement that provided we would drop to $1.25 billion
from $1.5 billion in cash from CGE in exchange for keeping the
STC shares, which had been put into the deal at $240 million but
had a market value at the time of $260 million. It was a good deal
for ITT. STC earnings were strong, and the declining dollar in
relation to the pound, plus the increasing stock price, boded well
for the value of the ITT holding. Ultimately, in October 1987, we
sold the 24 percent interest in STC for a whopping $730 million.

Our holding had tripled in value since it had been removed from the joint venture.

In those last days of December, when the 24 percent of STC stock was retained by ITT, our ownership in the joint venture went back to 37 percent. All primary shares were duly transferred. Standard Electrica's stock transferred in Spain, as did STK's in Norway. Only Taiwan, Sweden, Nigeria, two small Latin American holdings, and a small African one were put off for January transfer; $112 million was held back by CGE, with ITT's agreement, for those companies.

Pierre Suard and I felt that everything was in good shape for the end-of-year closing. On a long-distance call from Paris, he indicated that CGE wanted to name the new joint venture "Alcatel"; Roxane would become history. They had done extensive worldwide studies and felt that this name, utilizing the name of CGE's French subsidiary, would be the best in terms of image and in terms of marketing programs. I concurred. I had been concerned that after all the market studies they had been doing on a new name, they would come up with something like "Duosys." I liked Alcatel, which has a nice ring in any language, has "tel" in it, and fit well with our subsidiary names, such as Alcatel Standard Electrica, or vice versa.

That was my last conversation with Pierre Suard until the deal was done. The documents were signed on December 30, 1986, in Brussels. I had sent several of our lawyers and their spouses to Europe for the Christmas holidays so that they could be there to complete the final documents. The marriage was announced in the press on December 31. The monumental deal was done!

24

Once Is Enough

I just hate seeing things disappear, even our competitors. . . . You
have depressions, you have wars. You have every catastrophe known
to mankind. But your job, basically, is to survive.
— Michel David-Weill

Harold Geneen once told me, "Rand, when you get it
the right way, the critics will disappear." For the
moment, I felt we had it right. The fortunes of ITT had dramatically improved with the creation of Alcatel (ex-Roxane). For the
first time since my appointment as chairman, the corporation had
a surplus of funds and a much-improved balance sheet. The flexi-
bility afforded to us by these new riches was something to treasure:
We would be extremely careful as to how we handled all that cash.

Juan Cappello notified me that *Forbes* magazine had selected
ITT as the most improved conglomerate of 1986. A few days later,
I wrote Malcolm Forbes to say that we were appreciative of this
recognition: "In 1984 ITT had suddenly sailed into stormy waters,
far more stormy than we had anticipated. The going had been rough
for a couple of years. Now we are in good water, but we are not
taken in; we know the sea will not always be this way."

Early in January 1987, in Brussels, ABC, CNN, ESPN, and the
Public Television Network conducted interviews with me to be used

in conjunction with our press conference on the formation of Alcatel. More than 150 reporters gathered in the twenty-third-floor conference room in the ITT Tower on Avenue Louise. I began by explaining the background of ITT and the history of the Roxane negotiations. Then Pierre Suard took over and did a masterful job of handling a variety of questions on the future of Alcatel. ITT received broad and favorable coverage on the joint venture. The *Financial Times* called the agreement a ''genuine tour de force in industrial negotiation, a breathtakingly radical piece of restructuring that would never have been pushed through without dogged determination, a touch of luck and extraordinary persistence.''

In creating this significant international joint venture, there had been exchanges of stock in countries all over the world. There was also strong activity in ITT stock and in the new CGE stock, which traded on the Paris Bourse. This resulted in associated trading in the stock of Standard Electrik Lorenz in West Germany, STK in Norway, and STC in England. Throughout all of this, confidentiality was maintained, and there is no evidence whatever of any insider trading on the part of anyone in our corporation or the companies of Roxane/Alcatel. These complex, multibillion-dollar global transactions were accomplished without any individual or corporation profiting unfairly, here or abroad. Inside information was kept *inside*.

The disclosures concerning the insider trading of the infamous Ivan Boesky were just the beginning. The press had played up Boesky as one of the smartest investors of all time, one who had frightened corporations with arbitrage investments. Boesky had been in and out of ITT's stock several times. Now he was singing like a meadowlark. The chairman of the SEC, John Shad, had decried greenmail and the leveraging of America in 1984, but he had done nothing about it. He was now excited about the quiet success of Garry Lynch, chief SEC enforcement officer, and his staff, in bagging Levine and Boesky. Shad appeared on television to say that more shoes would drop.

Suddenly the "Yuppies," the young people on Wall Street, were publicly identified by Arthur Leavitt, chairman of the American Stock Exchange, as being too spoiled and too greedy. Shad, other regulators, and politicians would bemoan the lack of ethics among young people, but in the last analysis, the tone, the ethos, and the setting had been established by their seniors. In the search for fast money, leveraged buyouts, hostile takeovers, arbitrage, and junk bonds were the tools and techniques used by all the preeminent "white shoe" investment firms, from Kidder Peabody to Drexel Burnham. These firms were not managed by children, but by sophisticated financiers.

The handling of Boesky was not a good start for those who believed in harsh discipline. The SEC tried to explain, plaintively and unsuccessfully, why they allowed Boesky to sell out of his stock at a profit before his illegal activities were announced, leaving others to lose substantial amounts. The lame excuse given by John Shad was that the SEC was afraid of panic in the marketplace. For a man who had been cheating the public, Boesky had been let off lightly. Whether his subsequent study at a theological seminary was to atone for past sins or to prepare for a future career as a TV evangelist is premature speculation. The three-year jail sentence he received was roughly equivalent to what a petty criminal would get for car theft.

Unhappily, ethics in America have descended to a lower plane, accepted by a majority of the public. You can contribute $20 million to the Harvard Business School for ethics courses, as did John Shad, ex-head of E. F. Hutton, when he stepped down from the SEC. It may be a little late to start teaching ethical behavior to people in their mid-twenties. Or you can contribute a medical center or university library and put your name on it, but that is a kind of self-serving "edifice" complex. Ethical behavior can be taught only by example, not in classrooms nor by alleged philanthropy. Only if business operates honestly, produces worthy products and services, and treats employees and customers with respect, can we expect to improve the quality of society and the actions of the young. The young must realize that it is far more important to be of service to others than to be merely avaricious.

Opinion-makers bear much responsibility for extolling the raider-takeover environment. Reporters, who hitherto ignored or played down the importance of business and commerce, found a new and exciting area to cover. Raiders were treated as Robin Hoods, even though they were primarily interested in their own pocketbooks. Boone Pickens pulled so much wool over the eyes of sophisticated editors and reporters that he could have been called "pullover Pickens." People who should have known better lapped up his rhetoric.

It is particularly ironical that two of our leading newspapers, the *New York Times* and the *Wall Street Journal,* ran editorial after editorial supporting the raiders' goals. Of course, both newspaper ownerships had two classes of stock to protect family interests and insulate them from the marketplace and stockholder democracy. They could shout, "Down with entrenched management" from their fortresses, but I am bothered by their arguments that their freedom to print what they wish must be secured only to current owners.

Curiously, not everyone was making money in the long bull market. Look at the raiders' public shareholders: Jacobs acknowledged that Minstar's stock has not moved at all, and he described himself a failure when stepping down as CEO. Pickens has said that Mesa Petroleum may have to dip into reserves to pay the limited partners their annual dividends.

But it was not only the media that created the environment of indulgences—the Government also has much to answer for. President Reagan ushered in a period of undisguised patriotism accompanied by glitz and showmanship, promising far more than the economy could deliver. Although he campaigned against the size of the national debt, he left office with the nation saddled by deficits on the order of $3 trillion. In order to service those IOUs, the

United States is draining savings from around the world, since our citizens do not save enough to cover our own costs. We are, in short, borrowing money to maintain an affluent life-style that we no longer can earn. Our debt is increasingly in foreign hands, and now, with the low dollar, so is our equity. Any thinking American could ask what has happened to the once-richest nation.

Had the government taken the lead, had it had the moral courage to say no to extreme deficit financing, the whole raider-takeover era with its easy money and phony financing might not have occurred. John Shad could have jawboned, as could have President Reagan or Treasury Secretary Donald Regan. But Washington was a vacuum where everyone collapsed or stayed silent. The foolish merry-go-round is almost over, but we are not back where we started. A lot of broken bodies are lying around, and a number are among the missing. In addition, a group of new multimillionaires has no ethical reason to be so proud of themselves as they are, and we should not be so fawning over their charitable contributions. These multimillionaires will be offstage when the leveraged buyout bankruptcies drop the curtains on the failures of the money plays of the 1980s. And who will pay for the junk bonds that heisted the original purchase offers of the LBO dealers? Insurance companies, pension funds, and savings-and-loan banks. (Guess what? another taxpayer disaster to cover the Federal Savings & Loan Insurance Corporation.)

Did raiders and LBOs make American business "leaner and meaner," as the *Wall Street Journal* insists? I say no, it made it weaker and bleaker for the decade to come. When trouble comes, and surely it will, I wish we could bill this trouble to the sidewalk gamblers, whose ethics practiced ten years ago would have put them deep in the gutter of American public opinion. More than likely, most of that bill will end up with the American taxpayer and the workers whose companies fail.

Innumerable hours of productive work are lost every year by senior executives contending with hostile proxy fights and unwelcome raiders. We are in danger of reversing the meaning of industrial capitalism, which was created to produce jobs, profits, goods, and services. The financial world has its place, but if we allow it to manipulate, dominate, and control legitimate business interests, the tail will be wagging the dog. Stock markets are valuable institutions, but one cannot simply be ruled by the logic of the latest fillip in price.

Warren Buffett, a noted investor and chairman of Berkshire Hathaway, observed that when the "price of a stock can be influenced by a 'herd' on Wall Street with prices set at the margin by the most emotional person, or the greediest person, or the most depressed person, it is hard to argue that the markets always price rationally. In fact, market prices are frequently nonsensical." The financial and corporate worlds must take some steps to insulate business from the sometimes speculative and deleterious actions of the marketplace. If America is to concentrate its energies, and not be sapped by unproductive asset shuffling, it behooves the leaders from both sectors to come up with a new set of rules. If not, we shall continue to rearrange the deck chairs on the *Titanic* while we await the iceberg.

ITT's recent history offers a significant, simple lesson for corporate America, especially for that part of the business and financial world so in love with debt and leverage. It was, in the final analysis, the huge corporate debt that precipitated ITT's time of troubles. The company was such a large, powerful, well-regarded, highly connected multinational that we had the hubris to think nothing could touch us. We were, of course, wrong. American corporations are treading on thin ice, as is the federal government, if they think that debt does not matter and that the good times will roll forever.

Finally, the excesses of the current era have the potential for real and sustained damages to our political processes and our economic system. Dubious financial restructuring has hurt research and development, weakened local communities where industries were forced to close, and destroyed confidence in our businesses. If this raider era is not over soon, a sharp reaction may set in against these manipulators. Government, at the behest of an aroused public, may step in to control financial markets and business. Great confusion and frustration are likely to be followed by pendulum-swing actions that are detrimental to free markets and free people.

Government, business, and the public have some hard choices to make. The country can no longer afford to do everything it would wish; indeed, it can barely afford to maintain the status quo. Nor will selling off the country's patrimony and its natural assets solve our dilemma. Slipping growth and productivity, a tidal wave of imports, a debased currency—combined with a rising flood of debt and the lowest saving level in forty years—all pave the way to a lower standard of living. Unless we start to spend more of our energy and ingenuity on the basis of an industrial society, our children will certainly suffer.

Professor William Z. Ripley of Harvard, the leading authority on corporations in the 1920s, warned President Calvin Coolidge that "prestidigitation, double-shuffling, honey-fugling, hornswog-gling, and skulduggery" were threatening the entire economic system. *Plus ça change, plus c'est la même chose.*

There is no telling when the hostile takeover-LBO craze will abate. When it does, it will no doubt be due to a lack of pragmatic results and bankruptcies rather than legislated fiat. It probably will not abate before it causes a general market disaster. There is a twist in raider-propelled LBOs among public corporations that should attract far more interest from the SEC, FTC, and other regulatory bodies. For example, the raider calls, makes the Hart-Scott-Rodino filing, the company's stock rises as the arbitrageurs become players, and then the investment banking firm arrives at the CEO's door with an LBO plan, a nonrefundable bill for services, and a check to finance the LBO. The raider is paid off and debt is exchanged for equity, but what is forgotten is that taxes are no longer paid into the national treasury because of interest deductions on that debt.

Safeway, Norton Simon, Beatrice, and now Kroger and perhaps Pillsbury make up a long list of companies "forced" into LBOs. It's all too pat. Meanwhile, we deplore the chaos caused by Third World debt, even the failures in our savings-and-loan and farm credit facilities, and as we do so, we roll right along with LBOs, which create another potential rollover of debt to be billed to the taxpayer for future payment. This LBO music will stop only when the Government insists on a minimum of 50 percent cash equity in any LBO. Otherwise, debt is created, the taxpayers suffer the consequences, and bankruptcies cascade.

ITT certainly learned that the cost of debt is a limiting factor in the health and growth of a company. We learned the lesson the hard way. And we had to avoid an unfriendly takeover in the process.

If we escaped losing to an unfriendly takeover, was any benefit to the company derived from the battle? Well, just as my father's neighbors helped one another to thresh wheat back in the 1930s, so, too, the people of ITT and their colleagues banded together with a new and stronger bond to thresh the raiders. We knew we had to win. The ITT Wars brought us closer together, like soldiers in the trenches sharing a candy bar or a cigarette during a break in battle. We fought when the odds were against us. We won, and ITT remains one of the most exciting companies of the twentieth century. We hope to keep the wagon train moving into the twenty-first century and not have to think about making a circle again. Once is enough.

INDEX